RIGHTEOUS MIGHT

One Man's Journey Through War in the Pacific

Craig Siegel

Rochelle Publications

Rochelle Publications
8815 SW White Pine Ln.
Portland, Oregon 97225

Copyright 2011, 2012 Craig Siegel. All rights reserved.
www.craigsiegel.com

Second Edition
Published by Rochelle Publications

ISBN: 978-0-9836361-4-4 (Hardcover)
ISBN: 978-0-9836361-3-7 (Paperback)

Library of Congress Control Number: 2012900114

Printed in the United States of America

To all the brave men and women of the U.S. Armed Forces who served in the Pacific Theater.

Contents

"No matter how long it may take us to overcome this premeditated invasion, the American people in their righteous might will win through to absolute victory."

President Franklin D. Roosevelt
December 8, 1941

Prologue

New Guinea, 1944.

The moon has gone down and they're getting ready to come at us again. At the darkest time of the night. I can hear them out there, moving around. But where are they? The jungle can play tricks with sound. You really don't know if they're still far away or right on top of you. So you have to be patient. The machine gun is set up. Ammo cases are ready. The men are ready. My finger is on the trigger. We peer out into the dark.

And we wait.

I'm sweating. But is it from this blast furnace tropical heat or from nerves? The equatorial sun beats down on you all day, the rain soaks you to the bone, the mosquitoes eat you up, and the enemy comes at you at night. You sleep with one eye open, as they say. That's when you can get sleep, that is. No wonder everyone is jumpy, including me. I just hope that no one starts firing before they actually attack. That's a sure way to give away your position and get yourself and a bunch of other guys killed.

Movement off to the left. Maybe this is it. Or maybe it's just an animal scurrying through the brush.

Patience. Patience.

Some of the guys look calm, collected, together. Ready for anything. Others look like they're about to break. We all know what's coming, it's just a matter of when. I can see the tension on their mud-streaked faces.

Just breathe.

But even that's hard to do when you're tired, on edge, dreading the coming chaos of combat, and the humid air feels as heavy as a wet blanket. If there is such a thing as hell, this must be pretty close. I was just a happy kid from Chicago's north side. The worst thing I had to worry about was passing my high-school math final. What am I doing in this steaming jungle on the other side of the world, sitting in this muddy hole behind a machine gun, waiting to use it to kill men who are out there trying to kill me?

Movement dead ahead.

Here they come. Shouting, screaming, firing.

The whole line opens up. The squad springs into action. I pull the trigger and start firing into the night. I'm the gunner and my job is to shoot the gun. I try not to think about anything else. Shapes appear in the night. A lot go down, but more appear. Just shoot the gun. The rest of the team is responsible for making sure there is a steady supply of ammunition.

We have the gun set on free traverse and I spray the area in front of me with .30-caliber rounds. Tracers streak through the darkness. My squad is doing their job. When one belt of ammo is spent another gets slapped in with machine-like precision. Grenades and mortars are dropping all around. Ours? Theirs? Who knows? Screams in the night. I just keep firing. I am determined not to be overrun. Those bastards are not going to get behind me.

Another belt goes in and the gun spits death out into the night.

But they keep coming…

Preface

"A gigantic fleet... has massed in Pearl Harbor. This fleet will be utterly crushed with one blow at the very beginning of hostilities...Heaven will bear witness to the righteousness of our struggle."
Rear-Admiral Seiichi Ito
Imperial Japanese Navy
Chief of Staff of the Combined Fleet
November 1941

At 7:53 a.m. on the morning of December 7, 1941 Commander Mitsuo Fuchida of the Imperial Japanese Navy excitedly radioed the code "Tora, Tora, Tora," to Admiral Chuichi Nagumo, Commander-in-Chief of the IJN 1st Air Fleet, reporting initial mission success – that they had caught the U.S. air and naval forces at Pearl Harbor by total surprise. The first wave of 181 carrier-based warplanes launched from four Japanese aircraft carriers, Akagi, Kaga, Hiryū and Sōryū, swept out of the hills north and west of the harbor in a coordinated attack on U.S. airfields and the ships of the U.S. fleet anchored in the harbor.

A general quarters alarm sounded all over the island and American sailors, soldiers and airmen scrambled to defend against the sudden, unprovoked surprise attack. But by the time the planes of the second wave left two hours later, the U.S. military forces and facilities had been devastated. Eighteen warships, including eight battleships, the pride of the U.S. Navy, were destroyed or badly damaged. The attack destroyed 188 aircraft. 2345 military personnel and civilians were killed and 1247 wounded. The Hawaiian Islands braced for invasion.

Before the days of television and 24-hour continuous news coverage, people received their first reports of breaking news over the radio. On that fateful day, the first news bulletin was broadcast over the airwaves at 2:26 p.m. Eastern time on New York radio station WOR. It, and similar bulletins moments later on the other networks, was short and terse. An announcer broke in to the play-by-play broadcast of a football game between the New York Giants and the Brooklyn Dodgers (yes there was a Dodgers football team in 1941) with this ominous report.

"We interrupt this broadcast to bring you this important bulletin from the United Press. Flash. Washington. The Whitehouse announces Japanese attack on Pearl Harbor. Stay tuned to WOR for further developments, which will be broadcast immediately as received."

The broadcast then returned to the game. Except for sporadic news bulletins and speculative discussions on a few news and current events programs later that day, that was all most Americans heard about the unexpected event that would send them hurtling into the world-wide conflagration we know as World War II.

In Chicago, sixteen-year-old Leonard Gordon was enjoying a typical Sunday afternoon. He and a friend planned to get a 10-cent shoeshine and then go to an afternoon matinee at the 400 Theater on Sheridan Rd. As the brushes put a high polish on their shoes, the radio reported the attack. The boys looked at each other. Where in the world was Pearl Harbor?

By the time president Franklin Roosevelt addressed Congress the next day, asking for a declaration of war between the United States and the Empire of Japan, Japanese forces had also attacked U.S. forces in the Philippine Islands, on Wake Island and on Midway Island. The nation was at war. And Leonard James Gordon, just one of millions of American young men and women, was swept up in it.

It was a different time. The situation was black and white. We were savagely and deliberately attacked, and not by some vague and amorphous entity skulking in the shadows, like Al-Queda. There wasn't any slow but steady buildup of forces to combat the spread of Communism in a tiny, little-known country in Southeast Asia. We were attacked by the armed forces of a resource-starved militaristic nation that had been brutally expanding its influence and territorial control in the Far East and in the Pacific. And we were in the way. The nation, which had been divided into isolationist and actionist camps while the rest of the so-called civilized world was at war, was suddenly spurred into unified action. Across the country, young men in the prime of their lives prepared to fight.

This is Leonard's story. It is a small piece of a much larger chronicle that makes up the fabric of our great nation. It is the story of a generation of men and women who answered the call to arms to preserve their freedom and ours. They survived bombs, and bullets and diseases in far off places, and came home to resume their lives. But they can't survive the relentless encroachment of age. Fresh-faced teenagers who flocked to armed services recruiting offices then are in their eighties today. And that generation is too-quickly disappearing. At the time of this writing, there is only one other remaining member of Leonard's company, H Company, 1st Infantry Regiment, 6th Infantry Division.

Before they are gone we owe it to them and to ourselves to tell their stories, to learn the good and the bad that men can do, to understand what drove them to risk their lives for their fellow soldiers, and for us, and to understand the sacrifices they made. Perhaps we realize that our opportunity to hear these stories is fading and that's why there has been a marked increase in interest in World War II lately, not so much from the viewpoint of generals and great battles, but rather in the personal stories of the men and women who fought the war, from the frozen forests of the Ardennes, to the sweltering jungles of the South Pacific.

I first met Leonard when I was in college, about a year older than he was when he enlisted. I was dating his daughter, Susan. One evening, at their house, I noticed a picture frame on the wall in the den. In the middle was a photo of a much younger Leonard in his Army dress uniform and surrounding it were various battle ribbons and insignias. But what caught my eye, and my curiosity, were a Purple Heart and a Bronze Star.

I asked Leonard about his wartime experiences a couple of times, but he always limited his replies to a few casual remarks. I sensed that he was reluctant to talk about it. Then, one afternoon, after I had been married to Susan for several years, we were sitting in his home office with no one else around. I asked him about the Purple Heart. I mentioned that I had started writing, mostly short fiction, and wanted to sink my teeth into something bigger, something historical. This time, to my surprise, he started talking. I scrambled for a notebook and a tape recorder.

Leonard held me enthralled with a flood of memories of his life as a soldier in the 6th Infantry Division. He took me from his home in Chicago, to boot camp in Oregon, to the bloody jungle fighting in New Guinea and the Philippines. At that time I knew much more about the European Theater than I did the Pacific, and, as I later learned, for good reason. There is simply more material, written and visual, about the war in Europe. Every year in June there are programs on TV depicting the Normandy invasion. Evan a casual knowledge of the war includes the Battle of the Bulge. But I had only vague knowledge about the landings on Leyte and on Luzon, the largest invasion force of the Pacific up to that time. Perhaps this is a reflection of the mood of the nation during the war. Even though Japan attacked us and propelled us into the war, Germany was always seen as the bigger threat to our security. So the focus was always on the European Theater. The official war strategy was even termed Europe First. The official strategy was to check the Japanese advance in the Asia/Pacific Theater, concentrate on defeating Germany, then throw everything against Japan.

In the Pacific Theater I was familiar with names like Guadalcanal, Tarawa and Iwo Jima – Marine engagements – and I of course knew about the doomed defense of Bataan. But I knew next to nothing about places strategic to the New Guinea campaign like Buna, Lone Tree Hill and the Kokoda Trail, or those on Luzon like Devil's Stepladder, the Cabaruan Hills, and General Yamashita's Shimbu Line. As I dove into the research for this book, I learned that one reason for the relative obscurity of these Army campaigns is that, while General Douglas MacArthur was quite prolific at publicizing his accomplishments, the Marines overall had a much better public relations department. So their campaigns and accomplishments are better known. I heard about these places and Army campaigns for the first time as Leonard told me about them and others, and he described the actions that won him three Bronze Star commendations for courage under fire, one of which surely would have been silver but for a spiteful company commander.

I started transcribing my notes and recordings, but postponed the project for a number of reasons, most of which could be traced to lack of sufficient quality time. One thing led to another and my little historical project was shelved. It would be more than fifteen years before Leonard and I sat down again for another series of interviews, revisiting those memories. But the memories hadn't faded over those years and Leonard recounted them in vivid detail, filling in names, places and other information crucial to completing a comprehensive, compelling narrative.

Last year I set out in earnest to complete the project. I found that the Luzon campaign is well-represented in World War II literature, but detailed material on the U.S. campaign in New Guinea is much less prevalent. I have listed book and report sources, as well as a number of internet sources in the bibliography. I contacted other 6th Infantry veterans to help flesh out the soldier's-level impressions and experiences in these campaigns. Their thoughts are woven into Leonard's story.

As I reviewed my conversations with Leonard along with my notes from the other veterans, a pattern began to emerge – a pattern of similar experiences and feelings both then and now. These young men left their homes, their jobs, their schools, their families to take the fight to an enemy threatening their country. Most volunteered, some were drafted, but they all answered the call. They were thrown into a brutal, deadly, often dehumanizing world of jungle diseases, bullets, artillery shells and bayonet steel. It was a gruesome business, destroying an army of dedicated, fanatical warriors sworn to fight to the death. But at the same time it was an adventure like none they had ever imagined. There was a definite excitement in being a part of the massive movement of men and machines that was the World War II invasion army. None of the men I talked to enjoyed killing other men; they were compelled to "get them or they'd surely get us." But they swallowed their fear and they did it. They did it because it would help bring the war to a close. They did it so they and their buddies would stay alive another day. Looking back there is a deep, lingering sadness for fellow soldiers who weren't fortunate enough to make it home.

And there was something else that came through loud and clear. Something I saw in Leonard's eyes sometimes when he was remembering those times. Whether they openly share their experiences with us, or keep them buried deep inside, these men all have a profound and overriding sense of pride that they accepted the challenge and they did the difficult and dirty job that absolutely had to be done.

The 1970 film, *Tora! Tora! Tora!* is generally recognized by military historians to be a fairly accurate account of the attack on Pearl Harbor, by Hollywood standards at least. It depicts the events before and during the attack as seen from both the Japanese and American viewpoints. At the end of the film, Admiral Yamamoto is sitting with his staff as they hear the results of the attack. His aides congratulate him on staging a successful mission. Yamamoto is calm and thoughtful and says, "I fear all we have done is to awaken a sleeping giant and fill him with a terrible resolve." While there is no proof that Yamamoto ever said those words[1] that is precisely what happened. The attack on Pearl Harbor, especially coming as it did before the Japanese declaration of war, galvanized the United States. Practically overnight the manpower and industrial might of the country was thrown behind a massive military effort to defeat the Axis powers. Japan, even with its fanatical military spirit, simply couldn't withstand the onslaught of men and materiel that came pouring across the Pacific. But to defeat them, young men had to fight...and bleed...and die.

This is Leonard's story – but in a big way, it's the story of all the brave men of the 6th Infantry Division. The words are his. They may not be brimming with literary eloquence, but they are straight from history, and they are straight from the heart. They represent what he experienced or knew at the time to maintain the flavor and feeling of a first-person narrative memoir. I have put additional background information and insightful quotes and stories from other 6th Infantry veterans in italics and sidebars.

Craig Siegel
Portland, Oregon
2009

[1] *What Admiral Yamamoto actually did say regarding a naval war with the United States was a comment he made to a Japanese cabinet minister some time in 1940.*

"In the first six to twelve months of a war with the United States and Great Britain I will run wild and win victory upon victory. But then, if the war continues after that, I have no expectation of success."

While not as eloquent as the quote in the movie, this comment turned out to be equally prophetic. The naval battle of Midway, considered by most military historians to be the turning point of the naval war if not the entire war in the Pacific, was fought exactly six months after the attack on Pearl Harbor.

President Franklin Roosevelt's Address to Congress

December 8, 1941

Mr. Vice President, Mr. Speaker, Members of the Senate, and of the House of Representatives:

Yesterday, December 7th, 1941 -- a date which will live in infamy -- the United States of America was suddenly and deliberately attacked by naval and air forces of the Empire of Japan.

The United States was at peace with that nation and, at the solicitation of Japan, was still in conversation with its government and its emperor looking toward the maintenance of peace in the Pacific.

Indeed, one hour after Japanese air squadrons had commenced bombing in the American island of Oahu, the Japanese ambassador to the United States and his colleague delivered to our Secretary of State a formal reply to a recent American message. And while this reply stated that it seemed useless to continue the existing diplomatic negotiations, it contained no threat or hint of war or of armed attack.

It will be recorded that the distance of Hawaii from Japan makes it obvious that the attack was deliberately planned many days or even weeks ago. During the intervening time, the Japanese government has deliberately sought to deceive the United States by false statements and expressions of hope for continued peace.

The attack yesterday on the Hawaiian islands has caused severe damage to American naval and military forces. I regret to tell you that very many American lives have been lost. In addition, American ships have been reported torpedoed on the high seas between San Francisco and Honolulu.

Yesterday, the Japanese government also launched an attack against Malaya.

Last night, Japanese forces attacked Hong Kong.

Last night, Japanese forces attacked Guam.

Last night, Japanese forces attacked the Philippine Islands.

Last night, the Japanese attacked Wake Island.

And this morning, the Japanese attacked Midway Island.

Japan has, therefore, undertaken a surprise offensive extending throughout the Pacific area. The facts of yesterday and today speak for themselves. The people of the United States have already formed their opinions and well understand the implications to the very life and safety of our nation.

As commander in chief of the Army and Navy, I have directed that all measures be taken for our defense. But always will our whole nation remember the character of the onslaught against us.

No matter how long it may take us to overcome this premeditated invasion, the American people in their righteous might will win through to absolute victory.

I believe that I interpret the will of the Congress and of the people when I assert that we will not only defend ourselves to the uttermost, but will make it very certain that this form of treachery shall never again endanger us.

Hostilities exist. There is no blinking at the fact that our people, our territory, and our interests are in grave danger.

With confidence in our armed forces, with the unbounding determination of our people, we will gain the inevitable triumph -- so help us God.

I ask that the Congress declare that since the unprovoked and dastardly attack by Japan on Sunday, December 7th, 1941, a state of war has existed between the United States and the Japanese empire.

Author's Note

It has been over sixty years since World War II. It was a different time, a much different world than the one in which we live today. The enemy was clearly defined and it was easy to vent anger upon him. He was, to us, a mindless tool of a maniacal psychopath intent on putting all of Europe under the boot of the German Reich, or a brutal, fanatical Asian warrior intent on ruling all of Asia and the Pacific for the glory of the Emperor of Japan. And those warriors of the Emperor had committed the ultimate transgression of attacking us while we were at peace.

The American soldiers' references to Japan and the Japanese soldiers were often crude, derogatory and sometimes outright racist. I have attempted to maintain the genuineness of their comments without significantly softening the words they used except in a few rare instances. But the reader should keep in mind the time and the atmosphere in which these men fought, a fight to the death in hellish conditions against an enemy sworn to give their lives for the Emperor. These men bore no hatred or ill will against Japanese Americans or the civilians of Japan. Indeed, in the war's latter stages, Americans went to great lengths, even putting their own lives at risk, to try to stop Japanese civilians from committing suicide as instructed to do by their military and civilian leaders.

The American soldiers' hate and vitriol were directed toward the Japanese military and its system and code that turned ordinary men into fanatical, cruel beasts who committed horrible atrocities against both civilians and soldiers. Still, when the shooting and shelling stopped, they could sometimes -- not often, but sometimes -- see that they were just someone's son, or husband, or brother. And they often expressed grudging admiration for their tenacity, courage and military skill.

Maps

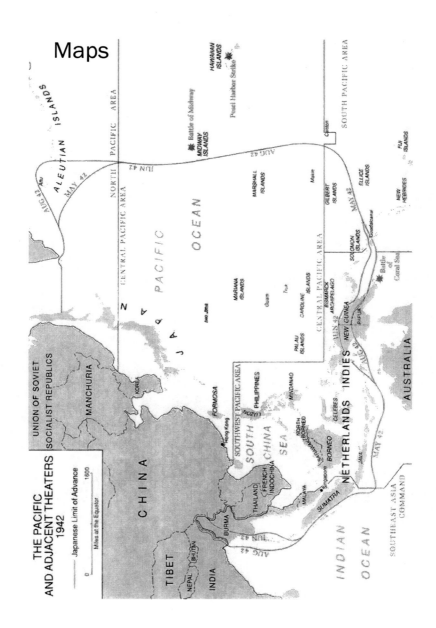

THE PACIFIC
AND ADJACENT THEATERS
1942

UNION OF SOVIET
SOCIALIST REPUBLICS

Japanese Limit of Advance

0   1600

Miles at the Equator

TIBET

NEPAL   BHUTAN

INDIA

BURMA

THAILAND

FRENCH
INDOCHINA

MALAYA

SINGAPORE

SUMATRA

C H I N A

MANCHURIA

KOREA

FORMOSA

Hong Kong

SOUTH
CHINA
SEA

SOUTHWEST PACIFIC AREA

LUZON

PHILIPPINES

MINDANAO

NORTH
BORNEO

SARAWAK

BORNEO

CELEBES

JAVA

NETHERLANDS INDIES

SOUTHEAST ASIA
COMMAND

INDIAN

OCEAN

PALAU
ISLANDS

CAROLINE
ISLANDS

Truk

Guam

MARIANA
ISLANDS

Iwo Jima

J A P A N

P A C I F I C

O C E A N

CENTRAL PACIFIC AREA

MARSHALL
ISLANDS

GILBERT
ISLANDS

MAY 42

ELLICE
ISLANDS

Makin

SOLOMON
ISLANDS

Guadalcanal

BISMARCK
ARCHIPELAGO

NEW GUINEA

JUN 42

PAPUA

Battle
of
Coral Sea

AUSTRALIA

MAY 42

NEW
HEBRIDES

FIJI
ISLANDS

Canton

SOUTH PACIFIC AREA

NORTH PACIFIC AREA

CENTRAL PACIFIC AREA

AUG 42

JUN 42

MAY 42

ALEUTIAN ISLANDS

Attu

MAY 42

AUG 42

Battle of Midway

MIDWAY
ISLANDS

Pearl Harbor Strike

HAWAIIAN
ISLANDS

xxiii

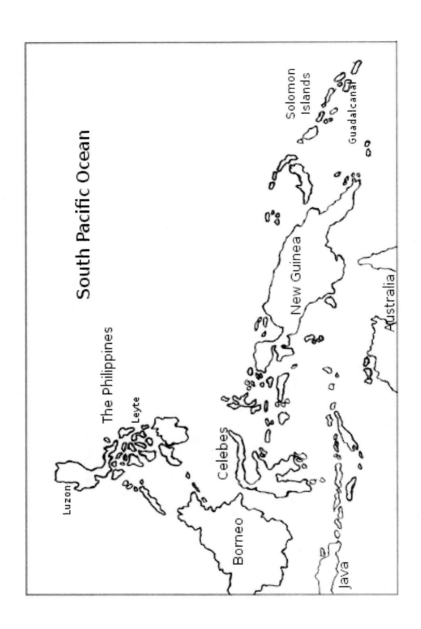

South Pacific Ocean

The Philippines

Luzon

Leyte

Celebes

Borneo

Java

New Guinea

Solomon Islands

Guadalcanal

Australia

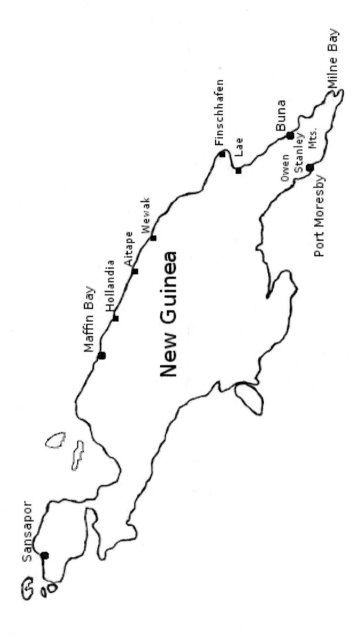

Milne Bay

Buna

Finschhafen

Lae

Owen
Stanley
Mts.

Port Moresby

Wewak

Aitape

Hollandia

Maffin Bay

New Guinea

Sansapor

Northern Luzon

Banaue

Baguio

Lingayen Gulf

Dagupan

Cabaruan Hills

San Jose

Munoz

Mt. Pacawagan
+
+Mt. Mataba

Bataan

Manila

1. Where's Pearl Harbor?

Looking back with the infallible benefit of hindsight, it's hard to imagine that anyone believed we could actually have stayed out of that damned war. Most of Europe had fallen, either through aggressive annexation or outright military invasion, under the control of Nazi Germany and its allies. Although we didn't know the depths of the depravity of Adolph Hitler and his Nazis, we had learned enough to know that Europe, and the entire world, was entering a dark and dangerous time.

The War had officially started in September of 1939 with Hitler's invasion of Poland, and by the end of 1941 the only major powers left fighting the Axis armies were Great Britain in the west and the Soviet Union in the east. And both were in trouble. We were officially neutral, but it was no secret where America's loyalties were. In March, President Roosevelt had begun the Lend-Lease program which enabled the U.S. to start shipping massive amounts of war material to England, Russia and China. Shipping convoys came under attack from Nazi submarines, further increasing the tension between us and Germany.

Most Americans were focused on events in Europe, but there were ominous developments in the Pacific as well. In response to Japan's invasion and war with China, the U.S. had curtailed shipments of raw materials to Japan. Proposals and ultimatums passed back and forth across the Pacific, reaching a climax the first week of December, 1941.

Still, most of the country was focused on Europe.

I was a sophomore at Sullivan High School on Chicago's north side. I signed up for ROTC because if you did, you didn't have to take physical education – gym – and I wasn't really the Phys Ed type. And things weren't going very well in Europe. I figured if we were going to get dragged into the war, I'd better get some ROTC training. That worked out pretty well, except that you had to wear the uniform several days a week. I had a job after school, so I had to run home fast and change. I didn't live very close to school so I had to jog all the way home, take off the uniform so it didn't get ruined, and change clothes.

I had a job delivering groceries after school for 20 cents and hour. I also helped my father, Sydney, in his portrait photography studio on Sheridan Road. I cleaned the windows and floors for him once a week and helped out around the studio. Around Christmas time he'd get real busy and I helped out by washing the prints and doing the dry mounting and framing.

In addition to taking portraits, Dad sold this concoction he called Gordon Royal Retouching Fluid. Back in those days we could say it would do pretty much anything... clear up wrinkles, straighten your face out, whatever. It was made with turpentine and all sorts of resins. We mixed it up, put it in little bottles and sold it. He had some sort of deal with Kodak. They sold it under their label and we got a cut.

The retouching fluid cost about 20 cents to make a bottle and we sold it for $3.00 a bottle. So he made a tidy little profit on it. All the camera stores in those days carried that sort of stuff. Demand was pretty high. We were always boiling a pot of it. I guess it was pretty dangerous boiling all those ingredients. I kept asking him where he got the formula. All he would say is – Lithuania. I never did get the formula from him.

In the fall of 1941, the talk was all about the Germans. We didn't know anything about the holocaust that was taking place, but everyone said, "It's the Germans again. We should have finished them off in the first war." Then the Japanese started moving around in the Pacific. We had been selling them our scrap metal... all those smashed up cars you saw in the junk yards. When we stopped those shipments, everyone started thinking that something was going to happen.

My mother had died when I was seven. It was the Great Depression and work was hard to come by. Sydney traveled around Europe for a few years pursuing his photography work and I was dropped off with my mom's relatives in the London Area. We returned to the states long before the war in Europe broke out. Business was better, but America was still in a depression.

> *In 1941, a loaf of bread cost 8 cents, a gallon of milk 34 cents and ground beef 15 cents a pound. A car cost around $900 and a gallon of gas cost 19 cents. A carton of cigarettes set you back $1.29. $2000 a year was a good salary and you could buy a house for $7000. The minimum wage was 30 cents an hour.*

I was running around with Ernie Siegel, Jerry Riff and Teddy Casino. On Sunday, December 7, Jerry and I planned to get a shoe shine and catch a movie at the 400 Theater on Sheridan Road. The shoe-shine guys were putting a nice shine on our shoes and they had a radio playing. I don't remember what we were listening to, but I remember the news bulletin interrupting the broadcast saying that the American military installations at Pearl Harbor had been attacked by Japan.

Jerry and I looked at each other. "Where's Pearl Harbor?" he asked. We had no idea. To us Hawaii was some island way out in the Pacific Ocean. No one even knew where it was. When someone mentioned Hawaii, all you knew about it was pineapples.

*"War, as we know it, began on Sunday, Dec
7th at about 7:45 a.m. Hawaiian time. In Monroe,
Louisiana it was about seven hours later. But
everyone can now tell you what they were doing
when they heard the news. I was in a movie theater
on Desiard St. watching Top Sgt Mulligan.
Hollywood was producing many military movies at
that time, usually about a draftee in the Army.
When I came out, the news boys were selling Extras,
telling about the attack on Pearl Harbor. But no one
knew where Pearl Harbor was."*
        C. B. Griggs
        Monroe, LA

The next day, Monday, the teachers called everyone
into the assembly hall to listen to the president's speech.
Everyone was scared and no one knew what to say. Our
teachers told us that the important thing for us to do was start
conserving and collecting. Pots, pans, anything metal that
you didn't want would be collected for the war effort. Old
tires, anything that was salvageable was needed. Then at
lunch, in the lunchroom, representatives came around asking
if you wanted to by war bonds.

At first there were a lot of enlistments, but then it
slowed down. Of the guys I knew, I think I was the only one
who tried to enlist during that initial period. I didn't know
anyone in the neighborhood who tried to enlist either. I
would be the first.

Soon, though, the newsreels they used to show in the
movie theaters started coming in. They showed the aftermath
of the attack, and when you saw that, it got your blood
boiling. Then you wanted to go. You wanted to enlist to fight
the Japanese.

I figured that if I enlisted I'd get my choice of service.
The recruiters said that you could choose the Marines, or the
Navy. If you wanted to go into the Army you could choose

the Quartermaster Corps, the Signal Corps, or the Air Corps. In those days the Air Corps was part of the Army. So I figured I would enlist in the Air Corps. I put down that I wanted to be in the Air Corps and the recruiter told me that would be taken care of when I got to Camp Grant. That's where I would be going.

There was only one problem. I wasn't 18 yet. That meant that I needed parental approval to enlist. I took the papers home and told my father that he had to sign some papers for school. I thought I could sneak them past him. But he looked at them, then looked at me and said, "Uh...I don't think these look like school papers." And that was the end of that.

I tried again in March of 1943. I was in my senior year of high school. The recruiters said that if you went into any branch of the service, you'd get your high school diploma when you got out. All you had to do was produce a copy of your honorable discharge. I figured I would get an honorable discharge, but I went to the principal and asked him if I could get my diploma in advance.

"Why can't I get it now," I asked.

"Why do you want it now?" he replied

"What if I don't make it back?" I said.

"Well, then it wouldn't do you any good anyway, would it?"

My division teacher, Mrs. McElvane, tried to talk me out of enlisting. "Leonard," she said. "Don't do this. You are still young. You should wait until they draft you."

So I said, "But what if they draft me and I get put in the infantry?" Little did I know.

I brought the enlistment papers home and showed them to my father. I told him that he had to sign them. But he wouldn't do it. My brother Milton had died suddenly of scarlet fever when I was a young boy and he didn't want to lose another son. He was visibly upset and I dropped the subject. But I figured they were going to take me soon anyway, so I registered for the draft.

I turned 18 in April, 1943. I figured I would be going in, so I left Sullivan and got a job at a place called Guardian Electric, a defense factory, for five bucks an hour. That was really good money at that time. I worked the swing shift, 4:00 p.m. to midnight. Fitzgerald, a friend of mine from Sullivan, got a job there too.

Guardian made parts for machine guns – gun controls, pistol grips and the like. I worked in the inventory department. We brought up parts from the other departments that manufactured them along with parts made by other companies. We brought all the parts together and then they sold them. In the inventory department we filled out requisitions... we need more of this part or that part... and when we had it all together we packed it up for shipping. I worked there about three months.

I also worked as an usher at the State and Lake Theater downtown. There I was getting about a buck and a quarter an hour. We had to wear this crazy dickey and collar. I took a few home to show to my dad. He just shook his head and said, "What are you going to do with them, you're going into the Army."

In July, a week before I left for the Army the Guardian folks threw me a going away party. It was at this fellow Harry Hamlin's place. He was a friend from Sullivan and lived in a big apartment right off Lake Michigan. He wound up going into the service later on. His father was an ex-judge or something, a pretty big guy in Chicago. I remember that his father came in and said, "No drinking." I didn't care because I wasn't a drinker; I was only eighteen. But a lot of the guys at Guardian were older, most of them were 4F for one reason or another, and they drank more than enough to make up for it. A lot of the gals from Guardian came and it turned out to be a pretty wild party.

One of the gals got me off to the side and asked me to come with her. She said, "I'll show you what real love is." You have to remember that there wasn't a lot of monkeying around in those days like there is today. I told her she was right. I didn't know what real love was, but I didn't want to find out just then. "I think I have some time yet," I told her. I think she understood. All the girls wished me well and told me to be careful and come back. A lot of my friends were dating, but I didn't have much interaction with girls at the time. I was too busy working.

My father drove me downtown to the train station. I was excited. He was sad and angry all at the same time. He thought that I could have stayed out of the service a lot longer. I told him that I was pretty sure I'd have to go anyway, but that didn't make things any better. When he found out I was going to be in the infantry, he was even more upset.

Camp Grant was in Rockford, Illinois, a couple of hours northwest of Chicago by train. It was a processing and training center. When we got there they said that after processing we would be going out to some camp on the west coast.

When you enlisted you were supposed to get your choice of service. A bunch of us had enlisted with the desire to get into the Air Corps., but we all wound up in every branch of the service except the Air Corps. At that time, in 1943, the demand for foot soldiers was far greater than the demand for anything else. We were losing our butts in the South Pacific, and the war in Europe wasn't going too well either. So they were forming different infantry divisions. We were sent to Camp Grant for placement.

First was a trip to the barber shop where you got your buzz cut, and off to the medical guys for a physical. Part of the examination was an eye check.

This guy says, "Read these charts and tell me what letter you see."

"Letters?" I asked. "What letters? I only see colored dots."

He said, "You're color blind."

"Color blind? I'm not color blind. I can see red, white and blue."

He said, "That doesn't mean a thing. If you can't distinguish letters in this chart then you are color blind."

"But I want to get into the Air Corps, or maybe the signal corps."

He was firm but understanding. "Look, your IQ is pretty good. Maybe that will get you into something."

That was a surprise to me. They had given everyone a test to see where you would fit best in the Army. I had guessed on a lot of the questions on the test, but scored pretty well. My only consolation was that he told me that after basic training I could apply for a different branch of the service. He said my grades were high enough that I could apply for OCS (Officer Candidate School) but only after completing basic. Then I learned that they were assigning us to a new division, the 70th Mountain Division, being formed on the west coast. It still didn't dawn on me that I was going to be in the infantry. All I knew was that it was a new outfit.

I learned later that Ernie Siegel and Jerry Riff both got drafted right after I went in. Ernie went into the Navy, Jerry into the Army. Ernie fought at Eniwetok. Jerry went in late and served on Luzon but luckily didn't see any combat. Teddy Casino was going to enlist after I did, but he died from something before he signed up. I never learned what happened to him.

We got our uniforms and it seemed like everyone's was either two sizes too small or two sizes too big. Nobody had a very good fit. The only thing they were really interested in fitting properly were our shoes. Other than that, they didn't care too much.

Our first destination was Camp Adair near Corvallis, Oregon, although we didn't know the specific location at the time. It was a three-day train ride out to the coast in railroad cars that were little more than boxcars with benches and a sort of porta-potty. When the train stopped the local townspeople along the way offered us coffee and sandwiches. It gave you a good feeling, seeing them come out to the train. These were the people we would be fighting for.

I don't think I was really scared so much as wondering what I had gotten myself into. On the train I met this guy, Koval, a big husky fellow who had worked in a steel mill in Gary, Indiana. He had been deferred for a while because he was working in the mills, but eventually he was drafted. I was just a scrawny kid and he took me under his wing. He was an older guy, in his 30s and he looked out for me.

I think I was the youngest one in our car. I made friends with two other guys on the train, Johnny Coffer and Dave Weissman. Johnny was a big insurance broker and owned his own insurance firm. He and Dave were also older guys, in their late 30s. They were on the very edge of the draft age and had gotten the call because there was such a high demand for personnel. There were all sorts of professional people on the train: bankers, lawyers, but no doctors. Most of the guys were from professional-type, higher echelon jobs, so I figured there was a still a chance we could be going to be in the Air Corps. We all speculated on where we were headed and decided that we were going to California. A day before we were scheduled to arrive, they finally announced that we were going to Oregon to a brand new camp. We would be among the first troops there.

2. Basic

When we got to Camp Adair, it was beautiful. Adair was in the lush Willamette Valley nestled between the Cascade Mountains that ran north-south up the western third of the state and the lower-elevation Coast Range mountains that gave way to the Pacific shore. There was green everywhere – trees, shrubs, all sorts of plants – and the days were filled with bright sunshine under mostly cloudless skies. We didn't know it at the time, but we had arrived in July and it was the dry season. Soon enough the rains would come. Everything would still be green, but the camp would earn its nickname, Swamp Adair. In the Willamette Valley, we would find out, from October to May there are only two weather conditions. It's either raining or it's going to rain soon.

As promised we were the first troops to make use of the camp. The Army announced that we were going to be in the 70th Infantry Division. They must have had it all planned out ahead of time because all the guys I had been traveling with were to be in the same company, Company G. It was then that I finally realized that I wasn't going to be in the Air Corps. I went to the company commander and complained, but of course it did absolutely no good. They told me what they had told me at Camp Grant, that if my IQ was high enough I could apply for officer training – after basic. The way they put it to me was that this was strictly basic training. You had to go through 13 weeks of training and then the ones that qualified could apply for OCS. I wasn't exactly happy about it, but I was smart enough to know that it would do no good to argue. For the meantime I was a lowly private in the infantry.

We found out that the 70th was a mountain division. That's why they sent us to Oregon for training. They talked about teaching us skiing and mountain climbing so we were sure we were going to be going to Europe. That would be the only reason for this type of training. But we were to find out that the Army would live up to its old reputation. Guys who are cooks are made plumbers and plumbers are made something technical.

Basic training was scheduled for 13 weeks, but no one said anything specific about mountain training. Thirteen weeks was a long time and some of the guys figured if they screwed up bad enough they'd get kicked out. But the harder you tried to get out, the deeper you got in. So I thought, OK, just take the 13 weeks of training and everything will be fine. Then see what happens.

Our Drill Instructor was Sergeant Brown. He was a big guy, six foot six and weighed around 280. Regular army. Nothing but a shaven gorilla in clothes. He was a pretty tough guy, but fair, and he made sure that everyone toed the line. But he had one problem. He was drunk half the time. He came from some place down south where he used to make homemade hooch. He must have brought some of it back up with him because most of the time he was pretty loaded.

Brown was an expert in Judo and he was trying to teach us the art. Of course I was young and he threw me around a lot. One time he was holding on to me and he was telling the squad what to do in such situations. "If you've got to kick them in the balls, kick them in the balls." So I kicked him in the balls.

I thought he was going to kill me, but he understood that's what he told me to do. "Well," he said. "That was my mistake. I should have been more alert." After that, however, he stopped throwing me around.

One day Brown called me over. He said, "You're strong." It was a half-statement, half-question.

"Yeah," I said.

"OK. Go pick up that machine gun and carry it. Let me see how you carry it."

Being a cocky kid I grabbed it and said, "No problem. It's light." It was an air cooled .30-caliber machine gun and weighed I guess around 50 pounds. They gave us the air cooled machine guns first and later we got the .30-caliber water cooled models.

"Good," he said. From then on I was assigned to heavy weapons.

It seemed like most of basic training was forced marches with heavy loads. This did wipe out quite a few of the older guys, which, for some reason, we had a number of in my company. And we had been put in a weapons group for some reason so we had a heavier load to carry than the other guys in the rifle companies. It was hard to believe that they put the older guys in that type of section where you had to carry heavier equipment. But they did and these fellows had never been on a twenty-mile forced march with full loads. They couldn't make it. They would drop off and I'd pick up an extra pack or two and carry them part of the way to help them out. Because I was doing that, these older guys became sort of my guardians. They took good care of me and made sure I had everything I wanted in camp because they needed me to help them out.

"The day began at 5:30 a.m. with reveille. A bugler blew it at post headquarters and transmitted it to each barracks. You had 30 minutes to get dressed, go to the latrine and get to the front of the barracks to line up by squads for roll call. If you wanted to shave or shower in the morning you had to do it quick or get up before 5:30. Chow call was 6:00. During breakfast the barracks were inspected to see who didn't make the bed and for other infractions. By 7:00 you got your first orders for the day."
C. B. Griggs
K Co., 1st Infantry Regt.

Of course they taught us how to use a rifle. I had some experience, being in ROTC at Sullivan High School, and this gave me an edge over the other guys. It put me one leg up on the training and it gave me an opportunity to earn some extra bucks. The pay in those days was $31.50 a month. By the time the Army took out insurance, your laundry and other expenses you had less than $20.00 to last you the entire month. The pay was raised to $50.00 a month about the third or fourth month I was there, but with all the deductions you still wound up with around $25.00, and that didn't go very far.

A lot of the guys were professional people and had independent extra incomes. The money they were getting from the Army was just peanuts to them. It helped a bit when they raised our pay, and to supplement my income I used to clean rifles for inspection. I charged the guys anywhere from $1.00 to $2.00 apiece to clean their weapons depending on how dirty they were. If you didn't have a clean rifle, you didn't get a pass to go to town. I could knock out 20 rifles on a Friday night for Saturday inspection. Between the guys I helped with rifle inspection and the guys I helped out on the marches I had a number of guardians looking out for me…and some extra spending money.

At first they gave us Springfields which were bolt action rifles, the same ones they used in World War I. In addition to rifles, the rifle squads also had light machine guns and 60mm mortars. But every battalion also had a heavy weapons company with 81mm mortars and heavy machine guns. I was put in the heavy weapons company because I was young and strong. I guess they figured if you were young you could carry the stuff. I still had to qualify with the Springfield, however. Being a bolt action rifle you had to pull the bolt to chamber each round. It had a 5-round clip. But it was a dependable weapon and had been around since World War I.

They didn't give out any ranks in basic. After you made it through everyone was automatically made PFC (Private First Class). I was made an assistant sergeant for machine gun drill because of my ROTC background. It didn't do me much good, actually. The appointment was made by the company commander who interviewed each man to find out about his background and ability. I thought the ROTC was going to do more for me, but all it gave me was more responsibility as an "assistant sergeant," whatever that was.

We had guys from all over the eastern half of the country there, but I think most of them were from the south, and a lot were from rural areas. Some of the guys in my platoon came from real backwoods areas and a couple of them had, shall we say, a hygiene problem. Henry was a big guy from Arkansas who was so dirty and so smelly that one day a bunch of us grabbed him and threw him in the shower. Everyone took turns scrubbing him down with laundry soap. That stuff was pretty raw and he squealed the whole time. Another guy we called Little John also smelled pretty bad and also had an aversion to taking showers. We didn't give him the Henry treatment, but we did put the two of them together in the barracks.

A couple of the backwoods guys were used to going barefoot and they didn't want to wear their GI shoes. They wanted to go barefoot even on patrols and maneuvers. Sergeant Brown told them, "Go get a handful of gravel, put it in your shoes, and put your shoes on." Henry said, "Ah, that's more like home."

As we approached the end of basic training they said we would be given a furlough, but that didn't happen. Instead we went up toward Bend in central Oregon on maneuvers. We had three weeks of hard living off the land. This area is high desert, drier than the Willamette Valley, hotter in summer and colder in the winter, cold enough to get significant snowfall. That's where a lot of guys ran into poison oak. On night maneuvers you dug into the ground to form a foxhole. You grabbed at the roots in your way, and then you'd start scratching yourself. The next thing you knew you were covered with blisters. We'd go back to the camp hospital and soak it in some sort of solution. I think it was calamine lotion and it was the only thing we had to relieve the itching. On time I had taken my shoes and stockings off up there and I got it on my feet. I had it so bad I couldn't walk on them. But I guess every cloud has a silver lining. They sent me to the camp hospital and I got out of basic training for a week.

Actually I was unfortunate enough to get poison oak a couple of times. When I got it on my hands, Sgt. Brown said, "Don't touch any of your privates." But I told him, "Hey I *am* a private." He was nice guy, for a drill sergeant, but I don't think he saw the humor of it.

Gradually they started taking us up into the hills and teaching us some skiing and snowshoeing. We also received instruction in forest fighting – fighting in heavily forested areas. Then we were even more certain we were going to Europe, because the type of training we were getting had the flavor of what we imagined European fighting would be. And all the people coming back into the division, replacements and such, were coming from Europe. So we all thought that was where we were going to go.

We came off about 10 weeks of maneuvers and that's when they told us we were going to be transferred to another division. But they didn't tell us which one. Up until that time we thought we were going to be in the 70th Mountain Division.

During basic training we sometimes got evening passes and we'd go into Corvallis. Corvallis wasn't much but it had a USO there and the local townspeople really bent over backward to make us feel welcome. After all, we were the first troops they had seen. When we completed basic training we got weekend passes to go up to Portland.

When we went up to Portland we usually hitchhiked because no one wanted to pay the bus fare which was, I think, 75 cents each way. But if we stayed too long and were in a hurry, sometimes we had to take the bus back to camp. You didn't want to be late getting back because then you wouldn't get another pass the next time around. We came right in to downtown Portland on Friday evening and we'd stay over Friday night and Saturday night. The USO had cots so we could sleep there, and they had sandwiches and other food for the soldiers.

Sometimes the guys got into a little trouble on leave. I never did, although I did buy liquor and secure hotel rooms for some of the guys even though I was under age. Some of the older ones wanted to have a good time with the ladies, but they were too embarrassed to get hotel rooms. So they would drag me along and I'd get the rooms for them. They were putting up the cash and we had a good time in town.

I also got liquor for some of the younger guys. Oregon was a state-regulated liquor state. You had to be 21 to get a liquor card and I had just turned 18. But it was simple enough to get around that. All you had to do was go down to the state office with your identification and a couple of bucks and you got yourself a liquor card. With that you could get a quart of gin, a quart of bourbon, a quart of scotch, and two bottles of wine a month. It was rather cheap, but I could sell it to the other guys for four times what I paid for it. So I picked up a little more spending money.

Everyone had a pay book that showed your birth date and your enlistment date. So all you had to do was change your birth date. My birth date was in 1925 and I just turned the 25 into a 22. But you had to have your pay book when you got paid so I figured I would just tell them I lost mine on bivouac. It worked and they gave me another one. So I had the right book for the Army, and I used the faked one for buying liquor on leave. When we went up to Portland on the weekend and went to the state liquor store there would be guys waiting outside willing to pay up to $15 or $20 for a bottle of whiskey. They were usually a mix of young GIs, who I think just bought it because it was available, and underage civilians. Usually when you went to town you only had about $20 in your pocket for the whole month, which didn't go very far. So a little extra spending money came in real handy.

Right before we got the order to ship out they issued us new M1 Garand rifles. We had already qualified on the Springfields but we had to requalify on the M1. The M1 was a wonderful rifle. Unlike the bolt action Springfield, it had an eight-round clip that you fed in. It was semiautomatic and you could shoot as fast as you could pull the trigger. When the clip was empty it popped out and you slapped in another one.

After we qualified on those we moved on to bazookas. The bazooka was like a hand-held rocket launcher. Well, not really hand-held because you rested it on your shoulder. It took two men to operate, one to load and one to fire. There were some old junked trucks out in a field and they let us fire a few shots so you could really see what the thing did. There was also a cement wall and you'd hit it with the bazooka to see what it could do to structures. The guy who carried the bazooka tube was responsible for the thing. The guy who loaded it had to watch out because shell was propelled by a little rocket and flames came shooting out the back end of the tube when it was fired.

We had been at Camp Adair about eight months when one morning they called everyone out onto the quadrangle. They told us to report to the orderly room and there they said the magic word. Furlough. Most of us got furloughs, but only the younger guys. The older guys, the ones that they figured weren't going to make it through to the end, didn't get furloughs. They gave us 14 days at home and three days travel time each way, since for most of us it took about three days to get home by train. I had to first go up to Portland, then pick up a train with the mountain goat logo on the boxcars. It was a real whistle-stop train, making every stop going back east through the mountains of Washington State and across Montana. We were going to be traveling in those darn boxcars again. So I called my father and he wired me some money so I could take a regular coach. Still, we must have stopped 20 times a day before finally arriving in Chicago three days later.

When I got in to Chicago and got home there was a telegram waiting for me ordering me to report back immediately to San Louis Obispo in California. I said, no way. Officially I was still a private, so what could they do to me? Bust me? My father said that I had to go back or they'd put me in the stockade. I told him not to worry about it. I wasn't going to turn right around and spend another three days on a train going back. I ignored the telegram and stayed in Chicago for two weeks. After 14 days I made the trip back, but I went back to Camp Adair. I didn't want to spend the extra time making my way down to San Louis Obispo.

When I got back to Camp Adair I found out that there were a number of guys who did the same thing I did. There were about 600 guys who were being transferred to various divisions that were short and the colonel wasn't too happy with us. He came up to me and said, "Do you know you were AWOL?" I figured, OK, here comes the court-martial. "Where were you?"

So I gave him the story I had come up with on the way back. "Well sir, I figured we were going overseas and I wouldn't get a chance to see another woman for a long time."

"If you were going to Europe you'd see a lot of them," he said, snarling.

"Well, I didn't know where we were going to go."

"So what did you do?"

"I shacked up with this girl in Portland and spent the whole time with her. So I never got the telegram."

"That's mighty funny," he said. "Seems like every guy I'm talking to shacked up in Portland. You are confined to barracks until further notice. You have to stay IN the barracks. You are not allowed out. No more passes."

So the Army put us in the barracks there, sort of in quarantine. I don't know if they believed us or not but we never got any punishment over it. After all, it was a very believable story.

We were confined to barracks about three or four days. Then one morning, about 2:00 a.m., the 1st Sergeant came in and blew the whistle. "Pack up. You're checking out. You are moving out." Everyone loaded up on a train and we traveled down to Fort Ord in California, just outside San Francisco. Ord, we knew, was a replacement depot. For two weeks we didn't do much of anything except march around the barracks once a day for exercise. Other than that we just sat around wondering what was in the cards for us.

I had a cousin, Leah Baskin, whose parents lived out there. They had sold their business in Chicago and moved to the west coast. Her mother and father came to see me at Ft. Ord and brought me some homemade cookies. She told me that her son Dave was an officer and had been assigned to the Panama Canal Zone. She asked me, "How in the world did you ever get in the infantry?"

I just shrugged, "It wasn't easy." When they left I remember thinking, where is the Panama Canal Zone?

Once again, one morning about 3:00 a.m. they came in and blew the whistle. This time we loaded up on trucks and rode to the docks on San Francisco Bay. They put us on ferry boats and took us across the bay to Camp Stoneman, which was a port of embarkation. So I thought, I guess we're going overseas now.

We were there for two weeks too, but this time it was two weeks of hard training. Every morning we ran the obstacle course. They really ran our butts off, hardly letting us sit down for a second. No one really knew what was happening, but we figured we'd know soon enough. Some of the other guys I met there said they were going to the South Pacific. So I guessed I was going to the South Pacific too. But just where was that? I knew where the Pacific was, of course. But just what was the South Pacific?

One thing that bugged us was – why are they sending us to the South Pacific when just before we left Camp Adair they had issued us brand new winter equipment and mountain gear? We had the newest type of coats, special shoes, boots, all of it designed for a cold climate. When we got to Stoneman all of that equipment was taken away and put in a great big pile. I never saw it again. Someone said they had burned it. I couldn't believe it…brand new stuff!

One of the noncoms came around and said that we had to take maneuvers because we had missed the outfit that we were getting assigned to. So I asked, "What outfit is that?"

"Can't tell you," he said. "But they are in Hawaii."

"So we're going to Hawaii."

"Don't count on it."

The first exercise they gave us was the obstacle course, climbing rope, going through tunnels, and crawling through the mud with machine guns firing overhead. They had charges in the water that they set off to simulate mortar fire. It was a pretty dirty business.

It was hot as hell, but I still had some of my personal mountain gear with me, including this crazy blanket overcoat. When I went back to Chicago it was cold and they issued you clothing for where you were going. This thing was like a big brown blanket with brass buttons. I had packed it in my duffle bag and hadn't taken it out when we left Ft. Ord for Stoneman. I figured, ah, what the hell, it might be good to sleep on. So I just left it in the duffle.

At Stoneman they taught us night fighting, dagger throwing, and how to stab a guy on the right side of the back to kill him quickly. We also had real heavy bayonet practice, and hand grenade throwing. At Adair we got to throw one grenade, and that was a dummy. Here they were live grenades. A couple of guys got so nervous that they dropped them. It was a minor miracle that no one got blown up in grenade practice – at least not while I was there. On the knife course we used actual throwing knives. The instructor said, "Where you guys are going to go a knife might be very handy." He showed me a razor sharp knife. "Oh that's nice," I said. "It's always good to have a knife."

One more time, at 2:00 one morning, they came in and blew the whistle. "Your company is going." We got in line and they issued us three suits of fatigues and gave us all Springfield rifles. I asked, "Hey, what about the Garands? We had training with the M1. Why are you giving us these?"

"Right now we don't have enough M1s but we have plenty of Springfields."

Everyone was upset because we knew we were going into the infantry and here they were giving us these old antique rifles, World War I vintage. We knew they were good rifles, but they weren't Garands.

"This is your rifle and you'd better take care of it. You lose this rifle, you lose your life."

"Oh, that's great," I said. "When we left Camp Adair they took all these guns away from us." Then I noticed that they weren't issuing ammunition, so I said, "Don't we get ammunition for these things?"

"You'll get ammunition when you are ready to land."

Great.

Before we shipped out, we were also issued white mattress covers. I asked the guy distributing them, "I thought we're going into combat. We're going to have cots where we're going?" All he said was that we'd find a use for them. He didn't want to tell us what their primary use would be.

> "My group was told at San Louis Obispo that we were going to the 6th Infantry Division. The division had three regiments, the 1st, 20th and 63rd. One day one of the guys went over to the 63rd area to visit a friend and they were gone. Rumors started flying. One guy had called home and had been told that someone from the 63rd had called home saying he was on the way to Europe. Another said he had gotten word from a friend at Division headquarters saying they had gone to Attu in the Aleutian Islands. In due time we were told that the 63rd was in Hawaii...but that didn't mean we would be going there."
>
> C. B. Griggs
> K Co., 1st Infantry Regt.

We loaded up on boats and they took us back across the bay to a great big dock or warehouse. It looked to be blocks and blocks long. They got everyone together and called the role. Two of the guys that I had ridden out on the train with to Camp Adair, John Coffer and Jerry Weismann, were transferred out and didn't go overseas because they were too old. They were transferred to some assignment in the states. I didn't see them again until after the war. I was sort of sad to see them go.

When my name was called I followed the other guys through to the other side where there was a big Army transport ship waiting, the General Polk. There was a band playing and a woman singing "When We Begin the Beguine." I remember that song. Then we loaded up on the ship and I thought, my God, what a ship. Look at the size of this thing. I'd never seen anything that big. It was a luxury passenger ship built before the war that had been converted into a troop transport.

The problem was that they told us we were loading 14,000 troops onboard and there were only bunks for 10,000. "So some of you guys will have to share your bunks." That's when this guy Koval came in handy. I was going to make a stink, but he said to me, "Don't argue with them."

We got on the boat and everyone was staking out bunks. They were stacked five high. I figured I'd shoot for a lower bunk rather than having to climb all over guys to get to mine. But I got pushed around in the commotion and could only stake out a top bunk. I didn't feel like arguing any more. I just threw my duffle bag up there and hoped I could keep the bunk for my own. Then some guy started giving me trouble, saying he was taking it. Koval stepped in, grabbed the guy by the collar, and told him, "You touch him and I'll beat the shit out of you." The guy stalked off, presumably to try to intimidate someone else into giving up a bunk. Koval said to me, "If anyone bothers you, you tell me. I'll beat the hell out of him."

I didn't have any more trouble after that... from anyone.

So I crawled up over the other four guys. Guys started doubling up for bunks – you had 12 hours on and 12 hours off for shared bunks – but fortunately I didn't get a partner. Maybe Koval had something to do with that. We left California behind us, wondering what was in front of us.

"We left San Francisco on the transport ship the General Butler. It was a liberty ship holding about 5000 troops. I recall passing under the Golden Gate Bridge. It was a wonderful sight. But I was thinking, will I ever see this bridge again? I don't

think I was scared. Frightened, yes, wondering what
I was going into."
          Vincent Impallomeni
          C Co., 63rd Infantry Regt.

About the third day out we ran into some really rough weather and guys everywhere were heaving over the sides of their bunks, right onto the floor. Boy did I luck out with that top bunk.

The General Polk was a big ship. But since she was carrying more than her complement of troops, everything was set up on a 24-hour schedule. It was like living in a sardine can. I think if everyone had gone up on deck at the same time there'd be no room to move. Even the chow line ran 24 hours, but you only got one meal a day. I was on the first shift which was good because the food was a little better. Often it was "shit on a shingle," more formally known as chipped beef on toast. I don't know where they got the beef, but it certainly didn't taste much like the beef I was used to.

The problem was that I was on Deck 1 and the chow lines ran from the different levels all the way to the kitchen. The guys from the lower decks had to come up and go through us. When they got their food there was no place to sit and eat, so they ate standing up. Guys were eating everywhere.

Being so fully loaded there wasn't enough water for freshwater baths. So we took saltwater baths. They were OK, except after a while you get this sort of slick on your skin from the salt. And we were limited to one canteen of water a day for drinking.

The ship was armed, too. It had 5-inch guns on the bow and stern and a number of 40mm antiaircraft guns all around. So we felt secure that she could pretty well handle herself if we came under attack from the air. And it was a fast boat so it didn't need to travel in convoy. Still, we had a destroyer escort for the first week, all the way out to Hawaii.

But we only made a short stop at Oahu and then headed for the South Pacific. It was supposed to be a 21-day trip to where we were going. But we picked up two Japanese subs on sonar and there was an announcement that everyone had to go below. Then they said that they were turning off all the lights and extra power so they could get more power to the turbines. So the air conditioners were going off.

Great, I figured, we're going to all be down there and we're going to get torpedoed. But I was on first deck so I thought maybe I'd have a chance of getting out if that happened. You think about these things when you are crammed into a boat trying to outrun an enemy sub that would like nothing better than to send you to the bottom of the ocean. But they must have had that boat up to about 30 knots. The whole thing vibrated but we had to get away from those subs. There was no ventilation below decks and a couple of guys actually passed out from the heat and squalid air.

We finally outran the subs by swinging to the south. The Navy had charted just how far enemy subs would go and the captain made sure to go farther south than that... a lot farther south. We had to travel so far south that it actually got cold. We didn't have our duffle bags with us then and I wished I had that big blanket overcoat. But it was somewhere in the ship's hold and I didn't have a prayer of getting it out. As it was, everyone stayed pretty close together because we were freezing our butts off.

So instead of taking us 21 days it wound up taking us 36 days to get to our destination. By the time we pulled in to Oro Bay in New Guinea, the rest of the 6th Infantry Division – they finally told us that we would all be going into the 6th or 41st Division – had already landed.

The 6th Infantry Division was only one member of a much larger U.S. force that would participate in the retaking and holding of New Guinea. In addition to

Australian troops that were there since the start of the war, the U.S. Army divisions that fought in the New Guinea campaign were:

6th Infantry Division	*38th Infantry Division*
24th Infantry Division	*41st Infantry Division*
31st Infantry Division	*43rd Infantry Division*
32nd Infantry Division	*93rd Infantry Division*
33rd Infantry Division	*11th Airborne Division*
1st Cavalry Division	

3. Prelude to New Guinea

As Leonard Gordon was finishing high school and then suffering through the rigors of basic training, events were unfolding in the Asia-Pacific Theater that would decide the role that he was to play in the war. He heard snippets of news, or course, regarding the battles and engagements, and after enlisting there was a mountain of gossip amongst the troops, but he knew little about the strategies that were being played out on a global scale. Like most enlisted men in the Pacific Theater, in combat he usually didn't know what the bigger picture was, even for his own regiment. He knew what his assignment was in the squad and he did it. But as readers of history, it is incumbent on us to understand why he had to do what he did. Why did the Army decide on the strategy of island hopping? Why did our soldiers have to invade and occupy a list of malarial, fetid, often heavily-fortified islands that, to that point, few people in America had even heard of?

There was a reason, of course. A solid one. But to understand why we invaded New Guinea, Guadalcanal, Bougainville, Iwo Jima, and all the rest, we have to go back to the very beginning of the war. Back to a time when the seemingly invincible armies of Japan spread out across Asia and the Pacific like an unstoppable swarm of locusts. In Asia and the East Indies, they had occupied territories primarily for their vast resources. In the Pacific, they had occupied tiny specs of land in the Central Pacific to build air and naval bases as part of their extended defense perimeter, to protect the home islands from attack.

It became clear very early in the war that ground or sea operations without air support were risky, at best. In the Pacific war, air power was crucial. Airplanes protected convoys and attacked enemy shipping, bases and installations. It was impossible to simply transport an army and all of its supplies across the vast Pacific Ocean and attack Japan. Without intermediate bases, there would be no supply line, and without air cover, any such invading force would be decimated before it even reached Japan. No, the Japanese had to be pushed back, island by fortified island. We had to take those islands away from the Japanese so they couldn't use them as airstrips...and we could. Indeed, one of the bloodiest battles of the war was fought over Guadalcanal because we learned that the Japanese were building an airstrip there.

At the beginning of June, 1941, the rising sun flag of the Empire of Japan flew over an enormous expanse of territory. It occupied Korea, Manchuria and a good chunk of eastern China. It occupied everything and everyone within a border that stretched from Burma in the west, across all of Southeast Asia, south to all of the Dutch East Indies and the northern coast of New Guinea and all of the Solomon Islands, then northward to the Gilbert Islands, the Marshalls, and Wake, continuing north all the way up to part of Sakhalin Island and the Kuril Islands off the Russia's Kamchatka Peninsula. They even occupied tiny Attu and Kiska Islands in the Alaskan Aleutians – U.S. soil.

So we had to push them, step by step, all the way back to their own doorstep. But in the beginning the outlook was very, very bleak.

The Japanese Onslaught

The Japanese attack on Pearl Harbor was only the first in a string of spectacularly-successful lightning attacks across the Pacific and Asia. On December 8 they launched air attacks against American bases on Wake Island and Guam. Japanese forces invaded the Philippines and Guam on December 10. That same day, Japanese bomber and torpedo bombers sank the mighty British ships HMS Prince of Wales and HMS Repulse, virtually eliminating British naval support for Singapore and Malaya. Japanese forces invaded Burma the next day. On the 16th they invaded British

Borneo and on the 18th, Hong Kong. In the Philippines, General Douglas MacArthur's American and Filipino forces fought a losing defensive battle on Luzon. The British surrendered Hong Kong on December 25.

The Japanese onslaught continued into 1942. On January 11 they invaded the Dutch East Indies and Dutch Borneo. On January 23 they established themselves on New Britain and Bougainville in the Solomon Islands. On January 31 they began a siege of the British garrison in Singapore.

America's first response to Japanese expansion in what was termed the Pacific Theater took place on February 1, 1942 with an air attack by carrier-based planes from the USS Yorktown and USS Enterprise on Japanese bases in the Gilbert and Marshall Islands. But it didn't seem to make much of a dent in Japanese expansion. They invaded Sumatra on February 14, and on the following day the British surrendered Singapore. Japanese planes bombed Darwin on the north coast of Australia on February 19, and they invaded Bali the same day.

American carrier-based planes hit the Japanese base at Rabaul on New Britain on February 20, but two days later President Roosevelt ordered General MacArthur to evacuate the Philippines. The Japanese were even bold enough to sneak a submarine up to America's west coast on February 23 to lob a few shells at an oil refinery near Santa Barbara, California.

The Allies, represented by the navies of the U.S., Britain, The Netherlands, and Australia, fought a series of small engagements with the Japanese starting in late January and continuing through February, in the East Indies area, a triangle roughly defined by New Guinea to the east, Sumatra and the Malay Peninsula to the west and the Philippines to the north. But there didn't seem to be anything the Allies could do to stop Japan from seizing the entire area with its richness of resources.

In an attempt to halt the impending Japanese invasion of Java, the Allied navies attacked the large Japanese convoy, meeting it in the Java Sea on February 27. The ensuing naval battle was yet another significant defeat for the Allies, effectively ending Allied naval presence in the Southeast Asia/East Indies area. Java lay open and the Japanese invaded on February 28. The Allied land and naval forces fought on, but resistance inexorably drew back toward Australia.

In early March the British evacuated Rangoon and the Dutch surrendered Java. Japanese forces established themselves at Salamaua and Lae on the north coast of New Guinea. General MacArthur was evacuated, under protest, from Corregidor, the doomed American/Filipino island garrison just off the coast of the Bataan Peninsula. On April 9, the beleaguered U.S. and Filipino forces on Bataan surrendered.

The Allies Attack

Then on April 19, 1942, Lieutenant Colonel James "Jimmy" Doolittle's squadron of 16 specially-modified B-25B Mitchell bombers launched off the deck of the aircraft carrier Hornet to make their famous bombing raid on Tokyo. The raid surprised everyone, especially the Japanese military. While the raid itself did minimal material damage, it was a tremendous morale booster for America, which to that time had suffered only a string of defeats at the hands of the Japanese. It also caused Japan to pause and rethink their war strategy. They recalled a carrier group from the Indian Ocean and four air squadrons from various points to be better prepared to protect the home islands. The fact that Japan was open to air attack also contributed to the High Command's decision to abandon a formative plan to attack Australia in favor of Admiral Yamamoto's plan to attack U.S. held Midway Island. This would be an effort to deal a death blow to the U.S. Pacific fleet while expanding Japan's control eastward closer to the Hawaiian Islands, a decision that was to have most profound consequences.

But the Japanese continued to expand their territory. In late April they took central Burma, and on May 3 they occupied Tulagi in the Solomon Islands. On May 6, the remaining forces on Corregidor under General Jonathan Wainwright surrendered.

Except for a small force that would hold out on the island of Mindanao for a few more days, U.S. military presence in the Philippines had ended. The Japanese High Command was making plans for the invasion of Midway Island and Alaska's Aleutian Islands.

Australia still figured prominently in Japanese war plans. While there is no evidence to suggest that they ever had serious plans to invade the island country – they did consider it but decided they didn't have the manpower or shipping resources necessary for such a large-scale occupation – they definitely wanted to take Australia out of the war. To that end they needed bases from which they could attack Australia by sea and air. They set their sights on Port Moresby on the southeastern coast of New Guinea. From a base there they could attack Australia with land-based planes. And from a base on Tulagi in the southeastern Solomon Islands just east of New Guinea, they could disrupt crucial Allied shipping lanes.

The Japanese launched Operation MO, the amphibious invasion of Port Moresby, but the convoy was intercepted by a joint American and Australian naval force in the Coral Sea off the eastern coasts of New Guinea and Australia. There, for two days, on May 7 – 8, the opposing naval forces slugged it out, this time exclusively with carrier-based planes attacking enemy ships. This was the first naval engagement in history where the opposing forces' ships never saw each other. When it was over, in terms of damage inflicted the Battle of the Coral Sea was a tactical victory for the Japanese. But it was a huge strategic victory for the Allies. The Japanese were forced to abandon their amphibious invasion of Port Moresby. This was the first time in World War II that a Japanese invasion force had been turned back.

And, the Japanese had temporarily lost the use of two aircraft carriers, which left the Japanese carrier group on relatively equal footing with the Americans. This was to prove a crucial factor one month later. The Japanese sent a sizeable fleet toward Midway, a tiny atoll 1300 miles west of Honolulu. Their goal was to seize the island and lure the U.S. Pacific fleet into a decisive battle. They achieved half of their goal. The U.S. fleet came out to meet them 500 miles west of Midway. There on June 3-7, exactly six months to the day after the Pearl Harbor attack, the two fleets battled it out with planes and submarines. Both sides suffered heavy losses, but in the end the Americans dealt the Japanese a stinging defeat. From that point on, the Japanese would be on the defensive in the Central Pacific.

But they still had designs on Port Moresby and the Solomon Islands to carry out their Australia strategy. Having failed to take Port Moresby from the sea, they decided to take it by land attack. They deployed their invasion force on the north shore of New Guinea in the Buna-Goa area. From there they planned to march across the Owen Stanley Mountains that ran down the spine of the eastern peninsula of New Guinea and attack Port Moresby from the land side. The route they planned to follow was little more than a rugged, muddy footpath across the mountains called the Kokoda Trail or Kokoda Track.

The Australians had other ideas. They marched out of Port Moresby and met the Japanese in the mountains. In a series of vicious battles from July through September 1942, the Japanese pushed the Australians back. During the last week of August the Japanese attempted an invasion of Milne Bay on the extreme eastern tip of New Guinea to support the Port Moresby attacks, but that invasion was driven off by the Australians. The Japanese on the trail pushed relentlessly forward until they were in the hills above Port Moresby, close enough to see the lights of the city in the distance. But the Australians had taken a heavy toll on the Japanese. Seeing that his men were exhausted and short on supplies, and knowing that all reinforcements were going to the continuing battle raging on Guadalcanal, they were forced to withdraw. In equally vicious fighting over the next two months, the Australians pushed them back over the Owen Stanleys, all the way to their starting point at Buna-Goa, which by then was a heavily fortified base.

While the Japanese and Australians were slugging it out in New Guinea, the Americans and Japanese were slugging it out on Guadalcanal. American reconnaissance planes had detected that the

Japanese were building an air strip on the island, the eastern-most in the Solomons chain. From there, Japanese land-based planes could harass shipping to Australia. So America began its land war against the Japanese by landing troops on Guadalcanal, Tulagi and Florida islands on August 7 to check the Japanese advance, and then use the island as a base for their own attacks against Japanese installations. The campaign started out with engagements by two relatively small forces. But each side quickly reinforced its garrison and the drive to secure what the Americans named Henderson Field and the surrounding area grew to include three major land battles, five major naval battles, and almost constant air battles. The Japanese finally gave up the offensive in December and pulled out all of their forces by February, 1943. As with Midway in the Central Pacific, after Kokoda in New Guinea, and Guadalcanal in the Solomons, the Japanese were on the defensive in the Southwest Pacific.

In November, as the Americans were securing Guadalcanal, the American 32nd Division, formed primarily from National Guard units, arrived in New Guinea. They attacked the Japanese positions at Buna on November 16, while the Australians hit the Japanese at Goa. Although ill equipped, ill trained and thoroughly unprepared for savage jungle fighting, they attacked the Japanese positions. In a two-month campaign whose casualty rates were among the highest in World War II, they drove the Japanese out of Buna. By the end of January, 1943, the 32nd Division, along with the Australians, and with help from elements of the 41st Division that had arrived earlier that month, they drove the Japanese from the Buna-Gona-Sanananda triangle. Australia was secure...for the time being. But the losses in men and materiel had been so high that General MacArthur vowed never again to order a direct assault on a major fortified Japanese position. "No more Bunas," he said.

The Japanese, however, were in no mind to give up New Guinea, and they were certainly not beaten or finished as a fighting force. MacArthur still needed to oust them from the northern and western parts of the island to eliminate the threat to Australia and to secure bases from which he could continue his campaign to the Philippines and on to Japan itself.

The Allied Onslaught

U.S. *strategy in the Pacific involved a two-pronged offensive with Admiral Chester Nimitz and the Navy in command of forces in the Central Pacific sector and General MacArthur and the Army in command of forces in the Southwest Pacific sector. This split command was the result of the reluctance or inability of President Roosevelt and the U.S. Joint Chiefs of Staff to unify the command for the entire Pacific Theater under one of the two bitter rivals as had been done with General Eisenhower in the European Theater. So MacArthur and Nimitz, both of whom were strong-willed to the point of inflexibility, and neither of whom trusted the other, executed their strategies somewhat independently, but both with the ultimate goal of taking the war to the Japanese homeland.*

In March U.S. and Australian planes defeated the Japanese in the Battle of the Bismarck Sea, disrupting their attempt to reinforce their New Guinea garrisons. In April, a U.S. fighter squadron shot down the plane carrying Admiral Yamamoto, the architect of the Pearl Harbor attack. And in May the U.S. invaded Attu Island in the Aleutians to evict the Japanese from U.S. soil.

In June, Admiral Nimitz pursued his Central Pacific offensive to push back the Japanese defensive barrier with his Marines invading New Georgia in the Solomons. In August, young Lt. John F. Kennedy skippered PT-109 on its ill-fated mission to attack the Japanese off Kolombangra Island in the Solomons. September saw the U.S. Army capturing Lae and Salamaua on the north coast of New Guinea. As 1943 drew to a close, the Marines invaded Bougainville in the Solomons, Makin and Tarawa in the Gilberts and New Britain, a strategic island in the Bismarck Archipelago between the Solomons and New Guinea.

The American onslaught continued into 1944. The Marines in the Central Pacific sector inched ever closer to Japan, invading Kwajalein in the Marshall Islands while carrier-based Navy planes destroyed a major Japanese base at Truk in the Carolines and damaged the massive base at Rabaul on the northern tip of

New Britain. The U.S. Army leapfrogged up the New Guinea north coast attacking Aitape and Hollandia in April and Biak Island in May.

The 6th Infantry Division arrived on the combat scene the first week of June, 1944. Their job would be driving the Japanese from the airfields first near Maffin Bay on the north coast of New Guinea and then at Sansapor on the Vogelkop Peninsula on the far northwest coast of the island.

4. Into the Rising Sun

We landed at Oro Bay on the north coast of the eastern section of New Guinea called Papua at that time. We went over the side onto landing barges, LCMs. You carried your gear and duffle bag with you. They had docks at Oro Bay, but they kept the boats out in the bay in case of air raids. The big boats would be harder to hit out in the water than if they were at the docks. They could move out into the open bay pretty quickly if they had to.

From the boats, Oro Bay looked like a tropical paradise, lush and green, with palm trees swaying in the breeze. It looked even better than Hawaii. But after we landed we realized that it only looked good on the surface. There was a war on.

At Oro Bay we finally were assigned to regiments and companies. But we were all split up. Most of the guys that were in my 2nd Platoon at Camp Grant were assigned to the 6th Infantry Division, but when we got to New Guinea, they separated us. It seemed like if you knew someone, you didn't go into the same regiment or company with him. And if you were related to someone, they put you as far away as they could. I think they did that on purpose because they didn't want you doing something stupid for your buddy or a relative, and they wanted to limit the possibility of two family members getting hit in the same engagement. Getting split up that way made me a little nervous and I felt a bit alone even though I was surrounded by thousands of GIs.

So after landing, I was with total strangers. Most of the 6th Infantry guys had joined the Army at Ft. Leonard

Wood in Missouri and took their training there. Some of them were older guys that signed up because jobs were still scarce and the Army was a way out. When I was in processing they looked over my personnel sheet and saw that I had taken training in light machine guns. But they had plenty of light machine gunners. What they really needed were crews for water-cooled machine guns which were basically the same gun with a water-cooled barrel. So they put me in 2nd platoon, Company H, 1st Infantry Regiment in the 6th Infantry Division. The 1st Infantry Regiment was one of the oldest colors in the Army, dating back to the Revolutionary War. But I wasn't much interested in history at that time. I went to Company H, and reported to 2nd platoon sergeant, Travis Buchong.

"You're going to be in 4th squad because they need guys who can read and write," he said. "A lot of those guys don't have a high school education."

"So what does this mean?" I asked.

"Nothing. Just do as you're told."

After having spent some 30 days on the transport with no freshwater baths, we pretty much smelled like a bunch of billy goats. And we all had this slimy slick on us from the saltwater baths. Someone told us that there was this sort of swimming hole down by Battalion headquarters and everyone made a mad dash for it. There must have been 300 or 400 guys down there cleaning the muck off themselves.

There were a lot of old timers in the regiment. Like Buchong had said, a lot of them couldn't read or write, which wasn't all that uncommon at the time. My 4th Squad was made up mostly of a bunch of really nice guys from the South. I was the youngest by about eight or 10 years, and in those days those few extra years made the older guys look really ancient.

In a machine gun squad you had a squad leader, first gunner, second gunner, three ammo bearers and a jeep

driver. I was made first gunner right away because I was
younger and the first gunner had to carry the receiver – that's
the heavy part of the gun. Each water-cooled machine gun
had its own jeep and trailer. I think that's how it was laid out
for the European Theater, so that's what we got... even
though the jeeps turned out to be pretty useless in New
Guinea. We mostly used them on the beaches to haul
equipment and supplies. They did come in handy when we
got to Luzon, however.

So there were seven men in a squad, with one water-
cooled machine gun. There were two squads to a section and
two sections to a platoon. The heavy weapons companies had
two machine gun platoons and one 81mm mortar platoon,
each commanded by a lieutenant. The entire company,
including messengers, noncoms, officers, and assorted
company headquarters staff totaled around 180 men.

Rifle squads were organized a bit differently. Each
rifle squad had 12 men including the squad leader. There
were three squads to a platoon and three rifle platoons in the
company. The rifle company also had a weapons platoon that
had mortar section consisting of three 60 mm mortar squads
and a light machine gun section consisting of two light
machine gun sections.

A battalion had three rifle companies and one heavy
weapons company, around 900 men, commanded by a major.
The regiment had three battalions, 3000 men, commanded by
a colonel. And the division consisted of three regiments. Ours
had the 1st Infantry Regt., the 20th Infantry Regt. and the
63rd Infantry Regt. Along with the other units such as
medical, artillery and such, the total men in the division was
around 14,000 commanded by a major general.

Oro Bay was only a replacement depot for the New
Guinea campaign and suddenly one morning they called us
out and they took us a short way down the coast to Milne
Bay. We would be joining our division there. When we got to

Milne Bay, we went into a tent city that had been set up already by a division that had pulled out. I think that was the 32nd Division that had just finished up a major bloody operation at Buna. They were being reformed, and replacements and new equipment were coming in. Some of the tents were big enough for 10 guys and they had raised floors made from coconut planks which would come in very handy when the rains came.

We were all excited to see our first action and rumors spread with lightning speed, as always. We're going here, or we're going there. All we knew for sure was that we were going to a beachhead further west up the north coast of the island. At Milne Bay we had a lot of landing training, going up and down cargo nets carrying equipment. Most of the division had taken some jungle training in Hawaii, but we didn't get much jungle training in New Guinea because the Japs were still infiltrating. They told us that we had to be always on alert because the Japs were sending out patrols on a regular basis. And here we were with Springfield rifles with no ammunition. We had our bayonets and trench knives, though, and we did have a pretty heavy and secure perimeter by that time.

There wasn't really a sense of time at Milne Bay. None of the enlisted guys had a calendar, and you sort of guessed what day it was. Of course you always knew when Sunday rolled around because there were church services for those that wanted to attend.

> *"The heat was terrible. Being a few degrees off the equator, the sun was directly overhead. We had soap to wash our clothes, but nothing ever dried out completely. It rained almost every day. I had not been in combat yet, but already I had the feeling that I had the privilege of being with some of the finest men in the world. The thought of coming back home kept me going.*

> *"During this time we lived in two-man*
> *tents. Each man had a shelter half as part of his*
> *equipment and we snapped two halves together to*
> *make a tent. The tent was A-shaped, about six by five*
> *feet at the base. We mounded up dirt for the base*
> *because we expected it to rain just about every day."*
> C.B. Griggs
> K Co., 1st Infantry Regt.

We did get some jungle training. We went out into the jungle on 10- or 12-man patrols with our ammunition-less Springfields. What a joke. We'd go out in the jungle and walk around in circles most of the time. The biggest danger we faced was getting lost. The jungle was quite thick and the compasses we had brought with us, for some strange reason, refused to point north. Everyone said that sooner or later we'd see a dead Jap rotting away and you'd know he was killed by a previous patrol. But for a long time I never saw anything. Just jungle, and more jungle.

I ran into a lot of Australians at Milne Bay. There were a lot of Aussie outfits there and they sure were glad to see another load of Yanks come in. The Aussies were super friendly and great allies. They couldn't do enough for us. I felt bad when, later in the war, they were slighted by MacArthur.

Naturally they were great gamblers, always on the lookout for the next card game or craps game. And they were talented souvenir makers. They would take old bullets or artillery shells and make all types of model airplanes using the shells as the fuselage. The crazy GIs bought them as fast as the Aussies could make them.

> *The Australians had shown themselves to be*
> *a dependable, capable fighting force, turning back the*
> *Japanese drive on Port Moresby at the battles along*
> *Kokoda Trail, and the battle of Milne Bay, and*

playing their part in driving the Japanese out of the Buna-Gona-Sanananda triangle. But when MacArthur's American Divisions began pouring into New Guinea, the Australians increasingly were assigned to mop-up and background operations. The reasons behind MacArthur's handling of Australian troops are unclear, but many Australians felt that with a lesser participation as the war continued, they lost their power to affect the peace terms and post-war plans. They took this as a definite slight and gradually lost some of their admiration for MacArthur.

As you might guess there was also quite a market for whiskey, and the Aussies were selling Australian whiskey. In Australia a quart of Aussie whiskey would sell for $1.50 or $2.00. But in New Guinea some of them were getting as much as $50 a bottle from the GIs. The Air Corps was flying a lot of it in on their runs and some of the Air Corps officers made quite a bundle of money selling it. The Navy ships also brought some of it in with their runs back and forth to the States.

Home brews were all over the place. There were a lot of guys from the south and they were masters of the art. Several guys carried the different parts of the still and they assembled it when and where time permitted. It took about ten days to ferment the mash which was made from any fruit they could get their hands on, usually raisins, along with yeast and sugar. It was illegal but the company commander drank as much as anyone else and turned a blind eye to it.

Sometimes they got a native boy to climb a coconut tree and toss down a few coconuts. Then they traded with the Navy guys to get the yeast and sugar. If they didn't have parts for a still, they just cut off the top of the coconut, stuffed the raisins or other fruit in there, put in some water and yeast, and put it in a hole in the ground so the top was sticking out.

After about ten days it would start to shoot out and you knew it was ripe, or at least ready to drink. They called the resulting concoction raisin jack. Pretty raw stuff.

This being Papua, or British New Guinea, we saw the result of British colonialism. The natives there looked pretty decent. It seemed like the first thing the Brits did was dress them up in short pants and get them to form a marching band. It was sort of humorous. Here were these natives all dressed up and marching in the band. They didn't have bagpipes, but I'm sure if they could have found some, they would have taught the natives to play them. Some of the local tribes, however, were still headhunters and ran around with hardly anything on except body paint. We had heard about the native girls running around with their breasts hanging out. But the view didn't quite live up to our expectations.

Even though we had established a perimeter, there was still Japanese sniper fire all around it. There were also some grenade attacks and a few knee mortar attacks. But they weren't very accurate. They were mostly just to harass us a bit... try to keep us off balance. The snipers were more effective. Sniper fire at Milne Bay was only at night. The sniper would look for any movement or someone lighting a cigarette. It seemed like almost every day someone would get hit. I knew a few guys that got hit, but not that well. The guys that got hit, you just figured they weren't smart. I really think that was one reason I made it through the war alive, that attitude. Maybe it was nothing more than the invincibility or the stupidity of youth. I wasn't really afraid; I never thought I was going to die. The ones that thought they were going to die just seemed to wind up getting killed.

> ... *each Japanese squad has two men normally assigned to sniping missions. These have for their fundamental purpose distraction of the enemy from his main tactical effort. The patience of these snipers is almost incredible. They have been known to lie in*

> *wait for three days to fire a single shot, and they have*
> *no hesitation in firing even when they are certain to*
> *be killed immediately by retaliatory fire. They are*
> *adroitly camouflaged and select their positions with*
> *great skill. Fortunately, their marksmanship is so*
> *poor, that they rarely are effective at ranges much*
> *more beyond 50 yards.*
>
> *Soldier's Guide to the Japanese Army*
> *Military Intelligence Service*

Almost every night there were a couple of air raids. It usually came as soon as the moon went down. All the new guys, including me, were excited at the first one. We finally had some ammunition and we wanted to get out and shoot our rifles. The antiaircraft batteries would go off all over the place, but very seldom did they hit anything at night. Once in a while there was a lucky hit and a plane would come down. But it was so seldom, it hardly seemed worth all the effort and expended ammunition. The raids were mostly harassing raids anyway. They rarely did any real damage.

When the air raid siren went off, the first thing you did was figure out where the closest dugout was. If you couldn't get to one you dug a hole and hit the dirt. The raids mostly went after the supplies that were coming in at the docks, and that was a few miles away from us. So usually we weren't in any great danger.

The Japs would also go after a small landing strip that was being used for cargo shipments. There were a lot of Japanese submarines patrolling the area so it was safer to fly supplies in from Australia in C47s. The C47 was essentially a flying boxcar. It was an amazing plane. It could still fly with only one engine and half shot up. We couldn't believe that any plane could take that sort of punishment and still fly... and land.

We started training for the next landing, but they didn't tell us where it would be. They just told us to load up.

We'd load up and be all ready to go, and then they'd pull us back. Dry runs, I guess. Then one day they came around, collected up all of the old weapons and issued new ones. Since I was in a heavy weapons company and was one of the first in line, I got a .45-caliber pistol issued to me. But I held on to the Springfield too, because everything was expendable over there. You could carry just about anything you wanted.

We also had a lot of Thompson submachine guns and the squad leaders got those. But you could practically pick any personal weapon you wanted. Some of the guys were even trying to buy them off each other. There wasn't much of an inspection. They just wanted to make sure that everyone had a weapon... any weapon. We learned that the day before the beachhead, ammunition would be passed out on the boats. They would open the cases up and you would just take what you wanted. But you had to be careful not to take too much because it could drag you down if you got into deep water.

Milne Bay was where I did see my first dead enemy soldier. I was on patrol and we came upon this Jap that was just sitting by the trail, rotting away. I asked why someone didn't bury the guy. But the sergeant said, "Any of the dead, just leave 'em where they lie. The thing you have to learn is to be careful. They may look dead, but they can still be alive. Or they could be booby trapped."

The Jap probably had been dead only a couple of days, but he was already turning black. We learned very quickly that anything that dies in the jungle decays terribly rapidly, including human remains. I didn't get sick, like I thought I might. I certainly didn't feel sorry for him. But I didn't feel any particular hate for that guy either.

Our next stop was to be Maffin Bay in Dutch New Guinea, although we didn't know the name of the place until the day after we landed. Late in May we got the word to load up. This would be our first landing under fire. Everyone was excited. We all wanted to get in and join the fight. You were a one-man army and you were anxious to get up to the front. We figured, we were in the infantry and this is what we have to do. This is what we're here for.

What we didn't know at the time was that the Japanese at Maffin Bay were dug in much more than we had expected. They had caves that were miles long. When we started shelling or bombing them they just pulled back into these caves. No matter how hard the Air Corps or Navy hit them, it hardly affected them.

We loaded up on attack transports, APAs, for transport to the beachhead. They were a little larger than a liberty ship, had a regular hold like a cargo ship, and could hold a fully equipped battalion. We steamed out of Milne Bay in single file and traveled under black out conditions. The ships had antiaircraft weapons but they rarely did any firing. They relied on the other Navy ships to fend off any attacking Japanese planes. The big ships were good targets for the Jap planes but the Navy did a great job, moving up and down the convoy. I had traveled to New Guinea on a single ship, the General Polk, so this was the first time I had seen a convoy. It was pretty impressive, all the ships, transports, destroyers, cruisers, in support of the ground troops.

> *"On the way to Maffin Bay, this lieutenant called us up on deck and gave us some instruction regarding identifying Japanese planes. While were up there a plane swooped in near the ship. He thought it was a Jap plane so he swung his carbine off his shoulder and stated shooting at it. It wasn't until the plane passed by that we realized it was an Australian Bristol Beaufort torpedo bomber. Luckily that carbine was like a pea shooter against that plane and it didn't even dent it."*
>
> *Mark Bradigan*
> *H Co., 1st Infantry Regt.*

It seemed like we were traveling pretty slowly, compared to the General Polk. I think the trip up the coast took four days. On board we got instructions on what to expect when we landed. We saw some Jap planes in the distance, but none got close to us.

Finally, we approached the coast, the spot designated for our landing. We climbed over the side and down the cargo net ladder to the landing craft that would take us to the beach. They were small wooden craft. About 18 or 20 guys loaded into our boat. Some were loaded more heavily than others. Machine gun crews were loaded a little differently than the rifle squads. Your rifle, the machine gun and all the ammunition went down into the boat with you. I still had the Springfield, my .45, the machine gun receiver and several cases of ammunition.

I was so busy getting ready that I really didn't have much time to think about what we were about to do – land in enemy territory where there would be men with guns trying to stop you. Once we got into the landing craft we had time to think. But even though we were scared, we were super excited. Half of the guys were talking how they wanted to get to the beach and kill their first Jap. Others were hunkered down, scared out of their minds, some even whimpering. A few prayed.

While we were loading up, the Navy was still pounding the beach. The night before the entire sky had been lit up. The ships were going back and forth, heavy cruisers and battleships, pumping everything they could in there. It was an awesome, but comforting sight. We thought, after that, the landing would be a snap.

But the Japs were still shelling the beach where I was and the boats coming in. Two of them in my sector took what looked like direct hits. Just before we hit the beach I looked out and saw what looked like some GIs floating in the water. I tried not to think about it. I learned later that the Navy was trying to fish them out of the water amidst all the landing activity.

I went in on the second or third wave. We were being fired on by Jap mortars and antiaircraft guns that were lowered to fire flat trajectory. The Navy had bombarded the entire area for 24 hours with everything but the kitchen sink, and the Air Corps had bombed the beach with napalm so the entire beach area was completely burned off. We were amazed that anything or anyone could have lived through it. But there they were, firing at us. They had hunkered down in their caves and when the landings started, they came out to greet us.

In the landing craft, most of the guys stayed hunkered down. You could hear the shells passing overhead and you didn't know if they were theirs or ours....or both. The boat had a two-man Navy crew and was armed with a 20mm canon for antiaircraft protection. But the crew concentrated on getting us to the beach. Their job was to get us in and then head back for the next group.

The landing craft ran right up onto the beach and we jumped over the side. We had had lots of training runs, but this was for real. Everyone was anxious and I was surprised that we all made it over the side without incident. I guess we all wanted to get away as quickly as we could from that big stationary target. I took the machine gun receiver and the Navy threw the ammunition cases over the side, into the water. They were waterproof, for a while anyway, and my crew grabbed them and dragged them to the beach. Up and down the beach I could see the other personnel craft as well as LCMs that brought in heavier equipment and artillery pieces.

Our first job on hitting the beach was to dig in. Everyone was running all over the place. At first it looked like a disorganized mess, but the platoon lieutenants sent runners out to their platoons. They barked out orders. "Get these guys over here. Move these guys over there. Move up to this point here." The platoon leaders had their maps and coordination points where they had to be. But we didn't even know that we were on the beach of Maffin Bay.

Gradually we started moving inland, up off the beach and into what was left of the foliage. As we moved in, the riflemen were ahead of the machine guns and we gave them fire support. We had the machine gun set up in seconds and just started firing. We put it level and just cut a swath with a barrage of lead. The runner said more ammunition was coming so we shouldn't be afraid to use what we had. I kept firing, but in the back of my mind I was always afraid of running out of ammunition.

Back on the beach there were scattered casualties. First the casualties were mostly from accidents, but then the enemy started zeroing in on us. But we had to move in, drive them out. So you just got up and started moving, regardless of the incoming fire. I look back on it now and I can't believe that we did that, all of us, moving steadily into the enemy guns. I didn't see anyone holding back.

After about an hour on the beach, another airstrike pummeled the Japanese positions and then we really started moving inland. None of the guys in my squad were hit, but we were close enough to guys that were. It was a sickening feeling in the pit of your stomach to see a GI lying there dead, or hearing a wounded GI calling for a medic. But the officers had drilled it into us. "Do not stop. Just keep moving. Your job is not to help. There will be other people behind you to help. Even if it is a buddy or a good friend, do not stop. And if you get wounded, just lay there and wait for someone to come to you."

So we kept moving in. We moved in little jumps. We broke down the machine gun. The squad would send out a point man, first scout, then second scout. Then we'd move up and dig in. Move up and dig in. One thing we had to watch out for was having the riflemen get too far ahead of the machine gun. Then we'd run the risk of hitting our own guys or having the enemy between us, and we'd have to pull them back.

The mortar guys were back on the beach, firing from there while the machine guns were up front for direct support for the riflemen. We got our orders from the platoon lieutenant or from a runner. Other than that you were more or less on your own. No one was telling us what to do. We knew our responsibilities. As gunner it was my job to make sure that we got the gun going and that we had enough ammunition to provide constant support for the riflemen.

By the end of the day we had established a beachhead. And as the day ended and the firing stopped, I finally realized that I had just survived my first day of combat. If that wasn't enough to put your nerves on end, it got dark – and I mean dark – really fast. Even the moon went down early. For me, that first night in the jungle at Maffin Bay was the scariest night of the entire war.

Our orders were, as soon as we stopped moving we dug in. Since we had the machine gun, we had to dig a foxhole, or slit trench big enough for the gun and the crew. Ideally we had three guys behind the gun, one to fire and two to load and get the ammunition ready. We did three hours on and three hours off, but some of the other guys arranged their own shifts. So we dug in... and waited for daybreak. I don't think anyone got any real sleep that night. I know I didn't. But I thought, for all the confusion, it was a pretty well-planned and executed beachhead. I sure wished we had some more combat-experienced guys there, though.

The officers told us not to shoot unless we had to because it would give away our position. But there must have been thousands of rounds of ammunition wasted that first night. Everyone was shooting at everything and anything....and nothing. "Only shoot when you see the whites of their eyes," Goldsmith, our lieutenant, said. But I think everyone saw white eyes in the dark.

If you needed more ammunition, you had to send one of your ammo bearers back to the beach to get it. Or, you could wait for the company runners when they brought up bandoliers of ammo to pass out to the riflemen. Everyone was so green, and it was all so confusing. In the dark I was afraid that one of our guys would crawl into a hole with ammo and get his brains blown out by some startled, trigger-happy GI.

> *"When you wake up you lose your sense of direction. So our own men hit some guys during the first night, because they didn't know their directions. After that night we learned to put our guns out in front of us in the direction we were supposed to fire. Then, when we woke up, we wouldn't shoot somebody else in the foxhole next to us."*
> *Vernon Kahl*
> *C Co., 20th Infantry Regt.*

On that first day there was hardly anyone around who had made a beachhead under fire, so no one really knew what to do or what to expect. Everything was done strictly by what we were told by the officers who had been taught or read something out of a book. The officers we had were generally pretty good, but many of them had no first-hand experience. And those that did have experience had little or incorrect information about the Japanese that were opposing us. There were still tens of thousands of them holed up in caves. We were to learn that so far we had only run into handfuls or pockets of resistance.

The next morning we finally learned that we had landed at Maffin Bay. We also heard that the Allies had landed on the beaches of Normandy to begin the liberation of France. That was exciting news but we just knew we had a beachhead to establish. We started digging in and sending out patrols. Being a heavy weapons platoon, we were attached to E Company for fire support. Wherever they went, we went. The goal at Maffin Bay was to build another airstrip for emergencies. So we had to move into and secure the interior so the engineers could build the airstrip. We would set up a perimeter and patrol about 100 yards into the jungle.

Nights were dark, forbidding...and usually wet. Every sound, every movement outside the perimeter was potentially a Jap, or worse, a lot of Japs. Machine guns, BARs and M1s blasted away at the darkness, usually at nothing. If your foxhole filled up with water you either had to spend the night in it, or you laid quietly and motionless beside it. You didn't dare move or make a sound or you might attract the fire of a Jap or another nervous GI. And if one guy opened up, it was a pretty good bet that everyone up and down the line would open up as well.

> *"That first night at Maffin Bay we were just off the beach. There were six of us in a group of foxholes and we were trying to decide who would stand watch at what time. Suddenly we heard this tremendous racket coming from the beach. What the hell was it? Was it the Japs? Fingers twitched on triggers. But it turned out to be just the sand crabs coming up from the beach.*
>
> *"The next day we moved closer to the area around what would become known as Lone Tree Hill. The Japs had an escape route about a half mile back. We dug in. I was scared that night. I swear I heard something out there. We had the machine gun set up on free traverse and I started firing. Then everyone else up and down the line opened up. It was a real comfort knowing that your buddies were on either side of you, firing away. In the morning there were 12 dead Japs in front of our position, nearly cut in two. Maybe I heard them, maybe I didn't."*
>
> *Mark Bradigan*
> *H Co., 1st Infantry Regt.*

*"Nights are dark and full of strange noises.
We are at the edge of a dense jungle. I don't look
forward to the long nights."*
        Robert Damm
        1st Field Artillery

We had the beachhead secured by the third day and after that, things sort of settled into a routine. In those first three days at Maffin Bay, our regiment became combat experienced. We figured out what we had to do. We took casualties. We learned what to shoot at, and maybe more importantly, what not to shoot at. When we finally saw a map, we found that 1st Infantry was positioned at the Tor River bridgehead, just east of Maffin.

As soon as we had the beachhead secure a battalion of engineers started building the airstrip. They came in with bulldozers and started leveling all the palm trees that were left after the naval and air bombardments. Actually, they wasted no time, moving in even before the shooting stopped. The terrain was pretty level already and they didn't have to do much to it. After they leveled it they put down steel mats to make the airstrip. The strip was to provide a safe landing place for crippled planes that couldn't make it back to their base or carrier, and to gas up some of the B25s. Almost before the strip was completed, planes started coming in, either all shot up, or to be gassed up to make it back to Australia.

*

The jungle around the Maffin Bay beachhead had been pretty well leveled, but there was still a maze of caves and tunnels that the Japanese had dug and fortified. We quickly found out that the only thing worse than a gopher was a Jap with a shovel. On patrol, you'd come across a Jap and shoot him. You'd think you got him and then another one would pop up and start shooting at you. We learned to hate those damned caves.

In addition to their fortified caves, the Japanese had constructed defensive pillboxes. The typical Jap pillbox was dug out, fortified with coconut logs and camouflaged for concealment. Coconut logs turned out to be an effective defensive material because the wood was soft and would absorb a lot of punishment from rifle, grenade and mortar fire.

> In all the combat areas where the Japanese troops have been engaged they have shown great skill in the construction of fixed defensive positions....Wherever possible, installations are made strong enough to withstand artillery fire and aerial bombing...they [defensive structures] will be most adroitly camouflaged and connected by tunnels or trenches. Local materials will be used for the most part in their construction. Coconut logs and coral rock have been used most extensively and have proved very satisfactory, since they are strong and do not splinter dangerously.
> Soldier's Guide to the Japanese Army
> Military Intelligence Service

At Maffin Bay, most of the time when we came across these pillboxes, the defenders had already been killed either by naval or air bombardment, artillery attacks or previous patrols. When you got close to one you could usually tell if it was out of action by the smell because the odor from the decaying bodies inside it was horrendous. But you didn't feel safe until you gave the interior a blast with a flamethrower, tossed in a grenade or two, or raked it with automatic weapons fire. Otherwise you couldn't move past it without the fear that one of them would crawl out and shoot you in the back. Even then, no one wanted to go down into the hole. The odor was so bad you could hardly stand it.

Inside the perimeter it was pretty routine for almost a week. Everyone was excited, especially on those first nights. We'd be in our foxholes and nothing would happen. Then all of a sudden the noises would stop in the jungle and you knew something was out there. But maybe it was nothing but a wild boar running around out there. We'd open up on where the noise was coming from and in the morning you'd find that poor dead boar all shot to pieces.

The jungle always had sounds, birds mostly. There were a lot of cockatoos in the area. It was sad to see the number of those handsome birds that were killed by shelling and rifle fire. You got used to their squawking. But sometimes you could tell when the Japs were coming because the sounds would stop. If there were cockatoos around that usually meant that there were papaya trees around and we could get some fresh papayas.

Of course there were palm trees everywhere. Most of the trees in the combat area had been destroyed, but some managed to live through the bombing and shelling. A lot of them were owned by the Palmolive-Peet company and the Army told us to be careful about destroying any of them because they'd have to pay for them.

Then, on the night of June 12 we got our first true counterattack. It wasn't the all out banzai attack that we had all heard about. They just kept coming, all night long, in little groups. I think their plan was to harass and disorient us. We were still jumpy, to be sure, but we were a hell of a lot more disciplined than we had been on that first night.

We'd be in our foxhole. We usually dug two holes so we could move the gun from one to the other. No sense in making yourself a stationary target for a Jap bullet or mortar. With two holes they were less sure where you were. The machine gun ammunition had tracers to help you hit your target. But the Japs could also follow them back to where you were. In the beginning that was a real problem. Later, though, the ammunition came with orange tracers that didn't light up until the round had traveled about a hundred yards. We also had flash hiders on the machine gun barrel. The flash hiders didn't do very much, but the orange tracers were pretty effective.

The Japs always attacked at night. When the moon went down, when it got the darkest, they came. The birds would go quiet and you could hear the Japs jabbering. Our lieutenant said, "No one fires his machine gun until you can smell them. When you smell them, then you shoot them." They used to put on something that smelled like perfume, and sometimes you could actually smell them when they got close. "Otherwise you'll give your position away and they'll send a suicide charge against you."

> In combat the Japanese soldier is strong and hardy. On the offensive he is determined and willing to sustain sacrificial losses without flinching. When committed to an assault plan, Japanese troops adhere to it unremittingly even when severe casualties would dictate the need for abandonment or modification of the plan. The boldness and courage of the individual Japanese soldier are at their zenith when he is with his fellows, and when his group enjoys advantages of terrain or fire power. He is an expert at camouflage and delights in deception and ruses. Japanese troops obey orders well, and their training and discipline are well exemplified in night operations. On the defense they are brave and determined; their discipline is good and fire control excellent. In prepared positions the resistance of Japanese soldiers often has been fanatical in its tenacity.
>
> Soldier's Guide to the Japanese Army
> Military Intelligence Service

Between the 12th and the 18th we had attacks every night. They became increasingly intense and on the fourth night they really came at us. We figured that we must be making pretty good headway and they had decided they had to do something about it. They just kept coming at us, all night long. I saw a lot of guys get hit. You get this sick feeling when you see your own dead lying there and they are tagged, waiting for the graves and registration people to pick up the bodies.

"When you see a guy go down in combat, you just hope he's only wounded. But when the guy next to you gets it in the head, you know it's over. You feel sick and you feel like throwing up. And you get angry. You want to get the bastard that did it. It's the worst feeling in the world. But it wears off in a couple of days."
Mark Bradigan
H Co., 1st Infantry Regt.

Sound in the jungle seems to carry, especially at night. Sometimes it sounded like they were right on top of you and they would still be 100 yards away. They'd be yelling and screaming at you trying to get you to open up so they could zero in on your position. So we were patient, and we waited, until you could almost really see them. Then we'd open up. And the bodies would start piling up.

During an attack we just started firing until the ammunition belt was done and then we slapped another one in as fast as we could. Most of the time you couldn't really see anything. You just kept a steady spray back and forth. And normally you didn't see if you hit anyone, but you heard them cry out when you did. We were lucky. Our emplacements in New Guinea were never overrun. I think one reason for that was that we had a bunch of guys who were patient enough to wait for them to come.

"During combat you don't have time to be
scared when you're fighting for your life."
Gary Mendoza
A Co., 1st Infantry Regt.

When they came at us you started firing and you didn't stop until they were dead or gone. We had the two holes for the machine gun, and if we thought we had been spotted we moved the gun to the other hole. We just went back and forth like that. Sometimes you didn't dare get out of the hole, because the minute you got out they just seemed to know where you were. During the fighting guys were yelling, "There's something by that tree over there. Give me cover here. I need a mortar drop right now..." that sort of stuff. If you didn't have religion when you arrived in New Guinea, you got it real fast when the Japs were coming at you.

When it quieted down we could hear the moans of the wounded. They were dying out there and sometimes you weren't quite sure if it was them or our guys. You'd hear, "Hey Joe, hold your fire, it's me..." that sort of thing. Some of them sounded pretty good and it made you think for a minute. We were green and this was our baptism of fire. We may have been scared, but you had to keep your head straight. You knew it was them and we'd usually toss a grenade out there to silence them. In a way it was almost a humanitarian act to put them out of their misery.

"After a firefight the jungle just swallowed
up the Japs."
Gary Mendoza
A Co., 1st Infantry Regt.

What really helped us was that we had already moved a lot of equipment up and we had enough fire power to repel anything that came at us. We called in artillery support from the beach when we could, but we had to be careful. We had to be careful about firing into the trees because the shells would burst in the foliage and then the shrapnel would rain down on us as well as the Japs. So we learned to stay away from the trees during artillery strikes.

We had also set out mines in front of the perimeter and that stopped a lot of them. They weren't true mines, but rather homemade contraptions that we devised. One type was made by emptying a hand grenade box and knocking the bottom out of the box. We taped the box to something that was standing up – if you could find anything standing up – and took the safety pin out of the grenade. Then you stuck it in the box with a trip wire. When someone tripped it, the grenade would either pull out of the box or drop through. Either way it was pretty successful. We also had tons of barbed wire around, but for some reason on New Guinea we didn't use it much on the perimeter. It seemed like it was used mostly to set up stockades.

Headquarters wanted live prisoners for intelligence gathering. But live prisoners were hard to come by. My company didn't get any until the very end of the Maffin Bay campaign. Other companies brought in a few supposed Japs, but most of them turned out to be foreign laborers from Formosa. They had taken off when the bombardments started. Most of the Japanese preferred to die for the Emperor, and we were more than happy to help them on their way.

> *Surrender is considered a great disgrace not only to the [Japanese] soldier but to his family, and his religion teaches the Japanese soldier that it is the highest honor to die for his emperor. There have been a number of instances where Japanese troops in hopeless positions have fought to the last, and the wounded begged to be killed to avoid the ignominy of capture.*
> *Soldier's Guide to the Japanese Army*
> *Military Intelligence Service*

I never really hated them, like some of the guys did, but I didn't feel particularly sorry for them either. Just before we went into combat the Army wanted to get us ready for combat. They showed us a film called Baptism of Fire. It included some films the Japs had taken of the Death March on Bataan. It showed how they captured our guys and force marched them to Camp O'Donnell. Some of our guys were down on the ground because they couldn't walk any further and the Japs were shooting and bayoneting them. The Army figured that film would get you good and angry...and it did.

As soon as we established control over the beachhead – someone from headquarters would designate that "we own the beach" – we unloaded all our supplies and equipment onto it. Then we dug in and we sent out patrols into the jungle. Since my platoon was attached to E Company we went out with them on patrol. If the patrol got pinned down the first thing we did was move up the machine guns and get just beyond the riflemen and start spraying the area – heavily. Then we waited for the riflemen to come in to try to weed out anything that was there.

Organizationally, the smallest unit was a squad with one machine gun. We had two squads in each section and two sections to a platoon. When you counted the drivers, squad leader, section sergeant and platoon sergeant, each section had nine men. What the Army did with heavy weapons companies was take sections or platoons and assign them to rifle companies for fire power support. We never fought as a company. The rifle companies we were attached to had about 200 men each.

Orders came from the company commander down to our first sergeant, Rosenthal. Everyone called him Rosie. He was regular army, a big guy, and real nice with a happy personality...for a first sergeant. The first sergeant was the highest enlisted-man rank and he spent most of his time with the company commander and the other officers. We never bitched to Rosie about orders. We may have bitched among ourselves, but never to Rosie or the officers. We got orders like, "This is the plan. We're moving up this way. We want everyone to make sure he does his job and we shouldn't have any problems." We usually didn't get very much detail. We usually didn't the bigger picture, just what our squad or platoon was supposed to do. I don't think anyone really cared about the bigger picture anyway, just our job. Most of the time we didn't even keep track of what day it was.

I got to know a lot of the other guys in H Company. Some of the guys were really friendly, but I was always somewhat of a loner. Our aid man, the medic who would patch us up in camp or under fire, was Doc Mullins. He was an older guy – in his thirties anyway – from Missouri as I recall, a little on the chunky side. His family owned a farm there. Mullins had gone through pre-med so he thought he would be put in the medical corps. But they put him in the infantry as a medic. He was pretty handy with a scissors and he would do a little barbering on the side, charging a couple of bucks a head. Harold Vissher was also a farm boy, but from Michigan. He was a straight-shooting guy, no BS. Real nice. He was on the skinny side with blondish hair and was very family-oriented. When I told him my name was Gordon, he started calling me "Gordy" and the nickname stuck. Irv Cohen was another Chicago boy, Jewish like me. He was a company clerk at headquarters. Then there was Odell Adams and a fellow named Shenkel.

A lot of the guys had nicknames. Mark Bradigan was another machine gunner. He was a kid, like me, but a good stocky Irishman. He was another farm boy, but from around Buffalo, New York. They called him Yank because he was a New York boy in a division with a lot of guys from Missouri. The St. Louis Cardinals and the New York Yankees played in the World Series in 1942 and 1943, so Bradigan became "Yank." Jim Tropin was called "Speedy" for some reason. "Red" Ellis got his nickname from his bright red hair. A guy from West Virginia in mortars was called "Goat Mongol."

Lt. Goldsmith was our platoon leader. Actually he was 1st platoon leader and I was in 2nd platoon. But he was always giving me orders. I learned quickly that he was a big talker, but when the bullets started flying, he sometimes sort of disappeared. He didn't like me from the outset. Then again, he didn't appear to like anyone. But I suspect from the way he behaved and how he treated me that he was anti-Semitic. He used to come up to me all the time and say something like, "Ya know, there's a new detail coming up and you're going to be on it." I kept telling him that he wasn't my officer, but that didn't stop him from trying to order me around.

The other guys in the outfit told me to "report the bastard" to the IG, Inspector General. It was a captain who came around periodically. Anyone who thought he was being mistreated or taken advantage of could report it to the IG. But you never knew what would happen when you did. You could end up with more problems than when you started. So I never reported him.

*

New Guinea was all about perimeters and patrols. We set up our perimeter and patrolled outward from there. The rifle squad went out, and we went out with them. Usually two days out, two days back. We were given a designated area to patrol. One of the objectives was to try to locate the Japanese, and to capture some prisoner who could be interrogated back at Battalion HQ. Unofficially, there was a bounty schedule. Capturing a noncom would get you three days on the beach, out of combat. An officer would get you a week. Snag a high-ranking officer and they said they would give you a trip to Australia. So there really was an incentive to bring them in alive. But in addition to the fact that they preferred to commit suicide rather than surrender, some of our guys would shoot them on the spot rather than take any chances with them. You never knew if a guy with his hands up was only faking surrender. We did capture some guys, but after we sent them back, Battalion told us they were only more Formosan laborers. So much for easy days on the beach.

Other than capturing an officer, patrols had one goal. Find the enemy and kill him. On patrol we had full packs. We always had two or three K-rations and a couple of C-rations. Water was really scarce. When someone got wounded, if he was going back to the rear we took his canteens. On my hooks I carried two canteens. The water got hot, but it was still water and you needed it. The rest of my hooks were for ammunition clips for whatever personal weapon I was carrying, usually an M1 Garand or a carbine. I liked the Garand. It was heavier than the carbine, but had a lot better stopping power.

> *"The company night defensive perimeter was a series of foxholes making a complete circle maybe 200 yards in diameter, depending on the density of the vegetation. You needed a sightline between holes. Two men to a hole with HQ in the center. Most of the time both men were awake until 10:00 or 11:00. After that one man stood watch while the other tried to get some semblance of sleep. Battalion passed down a password and countersign each evening. Any noise, or anyone approaching would be challenged. Words usually contained "R" and "L" sounds which were hard for most Japanese to pronounce."*
> C. B. Griggs
> K Co., 1st Infantry Regt.

When the rains came, everything turned into a muddy mess. But that didn't stop us from slogging through the jungle looking for the enemy, crossing a myriad of leech-infested rivers and streams. We all said, "Oh boy, this is a great place to get out of." It was one big muddy hole. No one and nothing was dry during the monsoon season. Everything got wet. The Army issued us waterproof food bags and waterproof clothing bags, but everything still got wet...and mildewed. The cigarettes in the rations were often green from rot, right through their wax paper wrapping. Weapons rusted out from the dampness and you fought a constant battle to keep your weapons clean. No matter how much you cleaned and oiled them, rust and corrosion would find its way into them. I had a stainless steel knife I had bought on the ship coming over to New Guinea. It was guaranteed not to rust. But after a few weeks in the jungles even it was pitted.

> *"During the day it was impossible to keep cool. You needed to drink about three or four quarts of water because it was so hot."*
> C. B. Griggs
> K Co., 1st Infantry Regt.

> *"It rained every day. It didn't rain very hard, but it rained all the time. All of our holes got full of water... This happened for three weeks. We never had our clothes off. We never had our shoes off. What's the use! Everything was wet. It stayed wet. Our fingers shriveled up and turned white."*
> Vernon Kahl
> C Co., 20th Infantry Regt.

The jungle had a definite smell to it. It was like mildew, but it also smelled of wet greens and dying vegetation. I have never smelled anything like it. There were birds everywhere, mostly cockatoos. You could always hear them chirping in the jungle. The papayas were pretty good, but the bananas weren't really edible.

Ants were everywhere too. Some of them were a half-inch long. There weren't any poisonous plants but there was one that had a disgusting sticky substance on it. Then there was the ever-present jungle rot. There is nothing worse than jungle rot. Any time you had a sore or got a scratch you could get jungle rot. Just from carrying your pack, the straps on your shoulders, or the cartridge belt around your belly, or if you had your shoes too tight, would cause sores. Then you called the medic over and he painted you up with a violet-colored medication called Jensen's Violet to kill the fungus.

Our shoes were a real problem. In the beginning we had Australian shoes that had soles made out of some sort of paper because there was a shortage of leather. And they didn't last long in the jungle. They simply rotted off all the time and had to be replaced. In fact, a lot of replacement parts for our uniforms were Australian made, cartridge belts, fatigues, and such. They were all made to GI specifications, but the quality just wasn't there. They simply didn't have enough quality materials to work with.

Our footwear on New Guinea was GI shoes, not combat boots. And we had leggings, like in World War I, to protect us from snakebites. But the snakes in New Guinea were all constrictors. There were other things there that were poisonous, but not the snakes. There was a worm that grew about four to six inches long and was about as thick as a role of pennies. The thing sprayed some sort of yellowish liquid that burned and blistered if it got on your skin. We all had machetes and I was always cutting them up.

After we came out of combat if we had been pinned down for a couple of days or couldn't take our shoes off for some other reason, our shoes would be soaked. So we took them off, jammed two bamboo stakes into the ground and put the shoes upside down on the stakes to dry out. We sprinkled DDT powder in a circle around the stakes to keep the bugs from going into the shoes.

One item we got in New Guinea was totally useless – combat hammocks. They were designed to be tied between two trees. But how were you supposed to use the damned thing when there were snipers everywhere we were. No one wanted to make themselves a nice fat above-ground target. I decided I wasn't even going to keep the thing, but I did keep the mosquito netting which I used all through the war. At night I wrapped it around my face to keep the mosquitoes off it. It was a shame. Those hammocks looked like they cost a lot of money.

Maffin Bay was in Dutch New Guinea and the natives there were very primitive. We called them fuzzy wuzzies because of their big frizzy hair. Even communicating with them was difficult because we had very few people who could talk to them, other than a couple of Dutch settlers. The Army warned us not to touch them because they had all sorts of diseases. A lot of the men had distended testicles and the women's breasts hung down low. You could always tell when the natives were around. They weren't really afraid of us, but they tended to keep their distance. Some of them volunteered to do different things around the camp and we gave them food and cigarettes. They couldn't quite figure out the cigarettes though. They thought they were for eating and they tried to chew them. We told them no and showed them how to light them with matches. They never quite understood the concept but they did like the matches because they could make fires with them.

On patrol, as soon as the riflemen established a point we had the machine guns ready to fire. Often the patrol would get into an area that was so densely covered with foliage that you couldn't see what was in front of you. If we had a bad feeling about it we set up the machine guns and threw two or three belts of ammunition into it, spraying the hell out of it, just to make sure there wasn't anyone out there. If you heard anyone screaming you knew they were there. That's when the guys would get really nervous. They were out there....but where?

The Japanese had turned the Maffin Bay area into a fortress of underground caves. Some of them went for seven miles. They had all sorts of equipment stored in there including artillery and antiaircraft pieces. They rolled the big guns out, fired them off, then rolled them back in, so you could never tell exactly where they were. And they were back so far you could never be certain of getting at them. Some of the caves were so big they were like little cities, complete with well-equipped hospitals.

When you saw a cave you could never be certain that there wasn't someone in there...watching...waiting. When you saw those cave entrances you blasted away at them with everything but the kitchen sink, and you'd think nothing could be left alive in there. Then you'd move in and all of a sudden that same damned hole was shooting back at you.

The strategy we came up with was to seal off the caves with the help of the engineers. The caves had breathing ports for ventilation. We found those and sealed them off. That, along with hitting the entrance with a flamethrower or a satchel charge, often did the trick. Put a blasting cap on a 25-lb satchel charge and you had yourself a homemade cave sealer.

We went in to some of them. We went in maybe 10-20 feet or so and you could see that the cave wound around into the darkness. We'd throw a grenade back there and lay flat. Still, we never wanted to go too far inside because you never knew what you would find. Some guys who ventured further into a cave never came out. There were always stories about guys disappearing in those caves.

As we moved along, if you saw a cave the first thing you wanted to do was throw a satchel charge in there.

Sometimes you could see that they were watching you and they'd move back into the cave. We needed to get in close enough to place the charge, but you had to be careful because the Japs often had snipers watching the cave entrances. We had to deal with them first. We did have some bazookas that we could fire from a distance, but they didn't do anywhere near enough damage. There was no getting around it; we had to get in close to toss the charge. Sometimes we tied a five-gallon gas can to the charge, got on top of the entrance, then sort of swung it into the cave. The combination of the explosion and the gas fire sucked all the oxygen out of the cave. If any of them came out, we cut them down. It was cold-blooded, to be sure, but it was them or us.

> *"I manned a bazooka and a flamethrower. I still have nightmares about the Japs running out of their caves on flame."*
> Gary Mendoza
> A Co., 1st Infantry Regt.

We would have taken prisoners instead of gunning them down like that, but they just didn't want to surrender. We learned right off the bat that they preferred to die fighting and take as many of us with them as they could in the process. Sometimes they looked like they wanted to surrender, like approaching you in a group with their hands up, only to open up on you with a hidden submachine gun or grenades when they got close enough. Or they would booby trap their wounded or dead with grenades or mines. So we didn't take any chances. If we saw them, we had to kill them. After an attack we sprayed the bodies with machine gun fire for good measure. Nobody knew for sure, but at Maffin Bay there could have been several thousand Japs entombed in those caves.

Somewhere along the line I lost that Springfield rifle. We pulled out in a hurry one night and I forgot to grab it. By that time I had a .45 pistol and I had also picked up a Thompson submachine gun off a dead GI. In those days Thompsons had compensators which helped keep the gun from spraying bullets all over the place. In the jungle that's usually what you wanted, so ordinance had removed the compensators. They wanted them as spatter guns. But the Thompsons were corroding and rusting out so badly that it was hard to keep them functioning. After a while ordinance started collecting them and issuing what were affectionately called grease guns. These were submachine guns that looked a lot like a mechanic's grease gun. Hence the name. The grease guns were made of relatively inexpensive stamped parts. The only machined part on them was the barrel. It was an expendable weapon. In the jungle you could rarely see what you were firing at anyway, so the idea was to just use the grease guns to spray bullets everywhere, then toss the weapon away when it stopped functioning after a couple of weeks.

*

It was on a patrol at Maffin Bay that I took my first souvenir. A Jap patrol, around a dozen of them, charged us and we cut them down. After it was over we examined the bodies. Some of the guys were afraid to touch them, but I rolled one guy over to make sure he was dead, my bayonet at the ready. If he was faking I was ready to give it to him. I was looking for maps, papers, anything that could be useful for intelligence. But when I turned him over his helmet fell off and there was a Japanese flag, with all sorts of Japanese characters written on it, tucked inside. I took if off of him. I was thrilled. I thought, well this son of a bitch deserves it. He didn't have any papers, but I took his watch and wallet.

I wound up trading that flag down at the airstrip to an Air Corps guy for some better food. The food on New

Guinea was a big disappointment. It wasn't anything like what we had stateside or in training. After we landed we didn't have any hot food for two days. When the beaches were finally established each company set up its own kitchen at Battalion headquarters. And if you were on the perimeter they brought it to you in big round marmite containers to keep it warm. We got in line and the first thing we did was dip our mess kits into hot water, sometimes soapy, but not always, then we dipped the mess kits in fresh water. After 50 or 60 guys went through the line, both barrels of water were pretty gross. After we ate we dipped our mess kits into clean water for the next session of bad news.

When they couldn't get food to us, we ate C-rations and J-rations. The C-rations were manufactured in Australia and the cans were often rusted, inside and out. Even the best stainless steel seemed to rust out there in the equatorial heat and jungle humidity. But the rations were relatively edible. The cans contained dehydrated eggs that you mixed with water. But since drinking water was so scarce we usually skimped on the water we used to make the eggs and they were pretty dry.

When we were out of combat, they got us two meals a day. When in combat they tried to get you one, unless there wasn't too much going on. Then they tried to get you two. But it certainly wasn't anything to write home about. Breakfast was usually powdered eggs and dehydrated potatoes. Every once in a while we got baked beans. Then there was a hard bread that we called dog biscuits. It really was shaped like a dog biscuit. You could chew the stuff forever and it would never get soft. If you put some of the Australian bitter orange marmalade on the dog biscuits, they were almost palatable. We also had something they called tropical butter that was designed to withstand the tropical heat. It was sweet tasting, but the chemists did their job too well. It wouldn't even melt when we put it in a mess kit and took a blowtorch to it. Another food item that wouldn't melt was called the tropical bar. I was a chocolate concoction. One of the guys put it in his canteen cup and tried to melt it to make hot chocolate. The cup melted but the candy bar stayed solid. We thought, how can you digest these things if they don't melt? I gave most of mine to the natives in trade for a little work.

For dinner we had a lot of Australian bully beef. It came out of a long can, like a spam can. They claimed it came from bulls and it was as greasy as hell. Later on we found out that even the crocodiles wouldn't eat it and we cut way back on it. There was a meat-like substance, sort of like bologna, that we affectionately called donkey dick which we usually made into sandwiches with the dog biscuits. When you're hungry you can eat a lot of things you wouldn't even look at under normal circumstances. We just ate it and said, "Oh boy, food."

And there was always coffee, if you could call it that. It was usually so acrid we used to joke that you could use it to sterilize your mess kit. After a particularly nasty cup I kidded the cook, Bull Torres.

"Hey, what did you do, throw your Army boots in the pot to give it a little kick?"

"Why not," he replied. "They were good boots, but I needed to soften them up a bit. So I threw them in."

Once I asked him how he became a cook, because he didn't seem to have any tremendous culinary skills.

"Well," he said. "When I was inducted they asked if anyone had any experience in kitchens. I said I did and that's all they ever asked."

"Did you have experience in kitchens?"

"Sort of. Before joining the Army I was a plumber."

"How the Army fed us was dictated by the same criteria that dictated everything in the Army -- it depended upon the situation and terrain.

"Each company had a kitchen tent, around seven cooks, including the mess sergeant, and the equipment to cook and feed around 200 men. This included portable gasoline stoves and ovens as well as fuel cans of about 30 gallons each. Some were used for garbage cans, if needed, and others to wash mess kits in. These cans were filled about two-thirds full of water, put on a portable heater and brought to a boil. One was soapy water and two rinse, all boiling. If we were in an area cleared of enemy, the kitchen crew moved up and fed us at that spot. They transported the stoves around on a truck, and left them in place for as long as possible.

"Meals were served from the cooking pots into your mess kit, also known as a shit skillet, two oblong pans which fit together when not in use, but opened into two halves held together by a folding handle. For liquids we had a cup with a folding handle which when not in use was in your canteen pouch with the canteen inside. You stored your knife, fork, and spoon inside the mess kit halves, but we wrapped them to prevent noise. Some guys kept them, separated, in their packs. Mine was an aluminum one, stamped 1917. Those made after 1942 were polished aluminum, and lighter. The 1917 models were best because they were easier to clean. I did not eat from a real plate from September 1943, until December 1945, except on the troop transports.

"Materials for clean-up were an integral part of the kitchen. Normally there were four large cans set up in a row. The first was for leftovers, scraps or garbage, which was later burned, or buried. Next was a can of hot soapy water with two brushes since we worked both sides of the line. This was followed by two cans of hot clear water.

"If the kitchen crew could not get to us with the trucks and tent, they brought the food to us in insulated marmite cans, about four or five gallon

capacity. They loaded them onto a jeep and brought them as close to us as possible. Sometimes a platoon would leave, go back a few hundred yards, eat, and return. Then another group would do the same. Usually we did this after dark since what better target for the enemy than 200 men in a chow line.

"We had A-rations and B-rations. The A-ration, was what we had in the U.S. They included fresh or canned fruits, vegetables, and meats. They were normally served in camps or permanent posts. The B-ration was an altered A-ration, being dried or dehydrated foods, prepared by the kitchen, but served in the field by the kitchen crew.

"Then, of course there was the proverbial C-ration, canned meat, beans, etc. These were in cans about half the size of a no. 2 can. They came 48 cans to the box and would supply 16 men with three meals a day...sort of. We swapped potted meat, beans and wieners, beans and pork, and the hard wafers to get enough to eat. They could be heated in the can. The rations came with a couple of small can openers per box.

"An improvement was the K-ration – one box, eight men, one day's meals. K-rations contained coffee, canned ham and eggs, pork and beans, chocolate bars, cigarettes, hard candy and some dried fruit. They were packaged in a wax-coated box which could be cut up and burned producing a blue flame and very little smoke. An improvement over the K-ration was the 10-in-1. It was one box providing 10 men with one day's meals. This had beef stew, even bacon, dried prunes and raisins. This allowed more communal eating. K-rations came in by trucks and the platoon sergeant, or squad leader would do the arithmetic, and draw rations for his men. He might tell you to put a two or three day supply in your pack and carry it."

C.B. Griggs
K Co., 1st Infantry Regt.

So trading Japanese souvenirs for some better food was a very appealing idea. The Air Corps and the Navy both had better food than us poor foot soldiers, and they were always ready to trade some food for a souvenir. I traded my flag to an Air Corps guy, figuring that I would be getting more of them down the road.

After we established the beach we moved west along the north coast toward Sarmi. We often came across bodies of Japanese soldiers who had most likely been killed in the naval bombardment. The Japs carried off their dead, especially the officers, whenever they could, but they had to leave these guys. In our excitement some of the guys still wanted to shoot the bodies, they had so much hatred for them. We continued to send patrols along the coast and we set up the machine guns at the points. My squad set up on the banks of the No Name River on June 18 so we could keep an eye out for anything coming down the river. The trickiest part of that assignment was watching the tides. If the Navy dumped off your equipment on the beach, you had to move it before the tides came in and washed it away. The river was a murky stinking mess. Although it hadn't rained much when we landed, after a couple of weeks the monsoons hit. It started raining and then it was like someone turned on a faucet. Everything turned to muck and mire.

Storm fronts came through and then it would rain buckets. It seems like we had a bad storm about every other week. After the rain stopped, it was refreshing for about an hour. Then the humidity shot right back up and you were soaked again. And you had to watch your head for falling coconuts that had become dislodged by the storms. We had a couple of guys get beaned, sometimes seriously.

The beach was loaded with destroyed Japanese barges, trucks and other assorted equipment. Almost every day you picked up something as a souvenir and then the next day you tossed it away because you saw something better. In those days a Japanese flag brought big dollars from the Navy guys.

*

The biggest battle of the Maffin Bay campaign, indeed one of the bloodiest battles of the New Guinea campaign, was fought over a rocky coral lump that overlooked the airstrip. The engineers were already preparing the airstrip, but before the planes could land in safety, we had to push the Japs off what would become known as Lone Tree Hill. Just where the name came from is sort of a mystery. Some guys claim the name came from a single tree that was still standing after the artillery units and Navy pounded the hell out of that hill. But since the hill was still pretty heavily forested, the name most probably came from an Army map on which the hill was depicted with the drawing of a single tree. Regardless of where the name came from, to us it was a place of death.

> *"We had huge piles of ammo yesterday, now we have huge piles of brass shell casings. Even with all this bombing, shelling and burning, we are expecting a lot of resistance when we take the hill."*
> Robert Damm
> 1st Field Artillery

The Japs were entrenched up there and we had to get them off. They had constructed a maze of bunkers and fortified caves on the cliffs, in the ravines, and in the swamps between the cliffs and the beach. Before we arrived on the scene, the 158th Regimental Combat Team had tried to take the hill, but had been repulsed by doggedly fierce resistance. Our 20th Infantry commenced their attack on Jun 20 but the first attack was beaten back by artillery and automatic weapon fire with heavy losses. First Infantry secured the flank while 20th Infantry renewed their attack. They finally reached the top of Lone Tree Hill on June 22 after heavy fighting. Jap counterattacks were furious, but they were concentrated on the attacking units. Our units on the flank were hit less heavily.

The men of 20th Infantry on top of Lone Tree Hill were cut off from getting supplies and the Japs attacked them relentlessly. We sent a relief company to bring them supplies, but it was pinned down by heavy fire and the relief effort was only marginally successful.

At one point, Companies I and K from 1st Infantry tried to make an amphibious landing around the back side of the hill. They were exposed and didn't have any artillery support. The Japs hit the landing barges pretty badly. The troops in the ones that made it to the shore had about 50 yards of beach to cross before they had any cover. It was a mess, a slaughter. They had to withdraw.

My squad remained with E Co. protecting the flank and we continued to beat off Japanese counterattacks. We knew that 20th Infantry was cut off on top of the hill and that other elements of the division were heading up to reinforce them. Both sides were taking heavy casualties in nearly constant fighting. Finally, the grit and determination of the Americans won out and the Japanese resistance began to weaken. By nightfall on the 25th, Lone Tree Hill was ours.

Sixth Infantry Division took that damned hill, but we suffered heavy losses in that engagement. The airstrip we had fought so hard over was being completed even as the fighting was still going on. After the area was secured the planes started coming in, mostly B25s and pursuit planes. Later on we started getting B17s, the big ones. They came in from Australia in the morning, made their runs to Celebes and the other islands, then went back to Australia. They didn't want to stay overnight at Maffin Bay because we were still getting air raids. Some of the planes were shot up pretty badly. If the airmen were badly wounded they were evacuated to

Australia because we didn't have any first-class hospital facilities.

If the plane was too badly shot up they just came up with a bulldozer and pushed it into a big pile. They stripped all the useable armament off them and then scrapped the rest. We searched what was left in the junk pile for anything of value. I took a gyroscopic stabilizer out of one plane and experimented with putting it on our machine gun. It helped stabilize the gun, but we never used it in combat.

As the Maffin Bay engagement went on the number of enemy dead increased steadily, so there was no shortage of souvenirs. We had so many Jap Arisaka rifles that they weren't even in demand after a while. My squad was on the perimeter one day when a group of six Navy guys came up souvenir hunting. Being an enterprising young man I asked what they had to trade. They produced some cans of boned chicken and turkey and we pointed them to a couple of pillboxes that were directly in front of our position. The pillboxes had been secured, but from the stench coming from them we figured there were still some Jap bodies in there.

The Navy guys were really nervous, because being Navy guys they were wearing their nice blue shirts. And it was a bright clear day...perfect targets for a Jap sniper. Even though the perimeter was secure, we still ran into a sniper now and then.

They were looking for Jap swords or pistols, but we knew they wouldn't find any of those. Most of those were sealed up in the caves – that's where the Japanese officers left them – and the caves in the area had all been blown shut. There were probably some flags in there, but even though we were getting $50 apiece for them at the time, we didn't want to go into those pillboxes after them. Even though the Japs had only been dead a couple of days, the stench from the decaying bodies was already something awful. In the tropics it only takes a few days for the flesh to start to rot. And most of the flags were so bloody, we didn't want any part of them.

We told the Navy guys we would show them where they could find their own souvenirs. They thought that was the cat's meow. They were going to be able to take their own souvenirs off dead Japs. Even though we knew there was no one alive in those pillboxes, we made it a little more exciting for them by creeping up and tossing in a hand grenade. Unfortunately that really stirred up the blowflies and the maggots that were already covering the bodies. Then we told the Navy guys they could go in and take what they wanted.

These jerks crawled right down into those pillboxes. We listened to them rummaging around for a while. When they came out they were carrying all sorts of Japanese gear, canteens, mess kits, rifles, bayonets, one guy had a pair of shoes, most of it spattered with human flesh. Actually it got really disgusting. One guy came out with a half rotted Jap head that had some gold teeth in it. The skull was full of maggots. They all smelled horrible. The smell of rotting flesh really sticks to you. There's nothing you can do to get it off. Even washing doesn't seem to get rid of it.

The guy with the head took off his shirt and put the head in it. The he really stuck out like a sore thumb in his white tee shirt. We figured we'd better get him back to the rear before he attracted any more attention. The Navy guys were the happiest bunch. They wanted to know if they could come back with their shipmates, but we said, no, no more. I guess headquarters found out about it too, because not long afterward they issued a directive that Navy personnel were not allowed to leave the beach area.

The only things I took were personal belongings. I had a bunch of watches that I sold to the Navy for American money. Of course flags brought a good price. Sometimes I took personal wallets. Those were popular with the rear echelon guys. I took anything that was sellable and I amassed a tidy sum of money. But I didn't know what to do with it. If I got killed, no one would get it. You couldn't send it back home because all mail was censored. So I just held onto it. By the time the war ended I had over a thousand dollars.

One of the other guys, Johnson, took a little more than personal items. He was also a farm boy from Missouri, a nice guy, on the small side, a reliable ammunition carrier in a fight. When we got one of our rare beer rations, he would bite the bottle caps off with his teeth. But he went a little over the line when he started taking the gold teeth out of the Japs' mouths. After a couple of days in the tropical heat their mouths would open. He dug out the teeth with his knife or put his foot in the mouth and broke them off with his heel. There was flesh on them which brought all sorts of bugs. So he got gasoline from a jeep or truck that had a gas can on the back and set them on fire to burn off the flesh. Then he added them to his collection which he kept in a box, like a cigar box. It was pretty disgusting. He asked me if I wanted in on the deal, but I declined, telling him that I preferred to make money selling the souvenirs that I took off the Japs, not their bodies. That war was barbaric enough without resorting to those measures.

He said he was going to get rich on the teeth. He thought if he got enough teeth he could buy himself a new house and a new car and more. Those teeth, though, would come back to haunt him in the not too distant future.

We really enjoyed the food we got from trading. We shared it with the rest of our section, about 20 guys including the riflemen. We split it up evenly and even kept a few extra cans to send to the company commander, which we sent to him with our compliments. We thought that our little gesture might get us some favorable assignments. But when he came looking for us, he accused us of stealing the food. We tried to convince him that the Navy had given it to us, but I don't think he ever believed us.

So it went on, daytime patrols, nighttime counterattacks. It's a wonder anyone got any sleep. In that half-sleep state my mother came to me a couple of times at Maffin Bay, and then afterward, always during severe banzais. She said, "You will see daylight tomorrow." And every day in combat, as I awoke to another day, or watched the sun come up, I would say, "Thank you God, for letting me live another day."

> *The night attack is a favorite tactical maneuver of the Japanese. As a captured Japanese officer is reported to have remarked, "You Europeans march all day, prepare all night, and at dawn launch an attack with tired troops. We Japanese allow our troops to rest all day while we reconnoiter your position exactly. Then at night we attack with fresh troops."*
> Soldier's Guide to the Japanese Army
> Military Intelligence Service

At night we dug in in our foxhole along with the rifle squads. We used sandbags, coconut logs, foliage, anything we could find to strengthen our position. Even though the Air Corps and Navy had virtually obliterated the foliage in the area, it was already starting to grow back.

In the slit trench sometimes we hardly said a word, especially at night. Other times we talked, usually about what we were going to do when we got back home, or out of the Army. We talked about the cars we would drive. We talked about girlfriends and you couldn't tell – and didn't care – if they were stories or true. Most of the older guys were married, some had kids, but they didn't talk much about their families.

Of course we talked about the different types of food we were going to eat when we got out. Mark Bradigan was always going to get the biggest, juiciest steak he could find, no matter how much it cost. One night Harold Vissher said to him, "Why don't you just get the whole cow and eat it." Vissher was always talking about his farm back home.

When we were on the perimeter in our holes, the guys who smoked had a rough time at night. The last thing you wanted was to make yourself a target for a sniper with a match flare or the lit end of a cigarette. Sometimes when it was raining we covered the machine gun with a poncho to try to keep it as dry as possible. One night I was in my hole and I smelled cigarette smoke. It was coming from the machine gun hole under the poncho. Some idiot had hunkered down into the hole and thought it was OK to light up a smoke. Our first sergeant must have smelled it around the same time because he said in a hushed growl, "Put that damned thing out," accompanied by a few choice profanities.

It usually got deadly quiet before a night attack. Then you heard them jabbering, sometimes screaming and yelling. The Japanese officers were trying to get them hyped up for the attack. A lot of them were loaded up on sake as well. The Japs always had lots of sake, and we captured a lot of it at Maffin Bay. It came in gallon-size containers. The first ones we found had Japanese letters on them and we didn't know what it was. We thought maybe it was some sort of fuel for the trucks, but one of our interpreters told us it was sake, rice wine. As soon as we heard that, guys were fighting for it. I tried it but I didn't care for it.

If there was a moon up you could sometimes see them coming, but they usually attacked when the moon was down. Occasionally they sent up a star shell to illuminate the area. Then you had to freeze so you wouldn't give away your position. Sometime we would send up flares too to illuminate them. But that illuminated you as well. When they finally started coming, if we had artillery they would start pounding the areas, under direction from liaison officers calling in coordinates, in front of our positions.

When the attack started they came screeching out of the dark, always with fixed bayonets. The rifle companies would fix bayonets and we had the machine guns ready to just flip up on the bipod and start firing in seconds. And it was up to the ammo bearers to keep belts of ammunition coming. A belt of 250 rounds didn't last very long. Usually we couldn't see anything so we just traversed the areas with crisscrossing fire. Amid the guns going off you could hear them screaming out there when they got hit. But they just kept coming.

We made pretty good use of grenades too. With our grenades you pulled the pin which activated a fuse. We had two varieties, three seconds and five seconds, distinguishable by the fuse color on the grenade box. You pulled the pin and lobbed it; you didn't throw it like a baseball. The Japs had to activate their grenades by hitting them on something hard to detonate the firing mechanism. Sometimes you could hear them hitting them on their helmets.

The experienced guys told us not to wear any grenades on our pack clips because if it snagged on something and the pin got pulled you had to get rid of that thing fast or you were in big trouble. I thought that was pretty sound advice, but some of the guys didn't listen. We had one officer, a replacement, who had the pin of a white phosphorus grenade pull out on him. He couldn't get rid of it fast enough and he wound up getting burned pretty badly. White phosphorus grenades came out in chunks and you couldn't pull them out, you had to dig them out. It was burning, and water won't put it out. What happens is a small piece of shrapnel breaks the canister open. It starts burning right away and explodes itself.

We had banzai-type attacks everywhere we were. Then there were the snipers. They could be anywhere. Sometimes the snipers would infiltrate our lines before an attack. They could sit in the swamps, submerge themselves and breathe through a hollow piece of bamboo. So a lot of times when we went through the swamps we threw a satchel charge in there, just in case. They were 5-, 10- or 25-pound waterproof charges in a small sack with a fuse. The concussion from the blast usually made them come out of the water.

A lot of the older guys had premonitions – I'm going to get it tomorrow, I know it. But not many of the younger guys had them, at least not that they talked about. We were all brave – I'm going to kill so many Japs. But when the bullets were flying and the Japs were coming at us, some of them just dove for cover. I can't say that I really blamed them. I told the guys in my section, "Just do as I tell you and we'll make it through this."

Anyone who was wounded was taken out pretty quickly for medical attention. If a guy was killed, Graves Registration Office (GRO) took them out. We took one dog tag and GRO took the other. That was one branch of the service I would never want to be in. Those mattress covers the Army gave us before we shipped out were put to unfortunate use as body bags. That's why they didn't want to tell us what they were for. And we had rubberized waterproof food bags, with the last four digits of your serial number stenciled on them, for our personal belongings. If you were killed or seriously wounded they sent the bag home to your folks.

"I came to realize that death was real, and the guy you ate breakfast with in the morning might not be there at the next meal, that he might have a leg blown off, or be dead and swollen up from the heat and you had to carry him to the makeshift cemetery. It made you wonder whether dumb luck or divine providence, or both kept that from being you."
C. B. Griggs
K Co., 1st Infantry Regt.

There were times, like if we were in sustained combat, or GRO couldn't reach us for some reason, that we had to temporarily bury our own guys. That was one tough assignment, one you don't ever forget.

> *"We had to bury our people, our buddies... I helped take off his dog tags, his rifle belt, and wrapped him in a shelter half and put him in a hole. I covered him up and put a cross by his head. The dog tags were wrapped around the cross; finally the belt and helmet are put on top... This is just one of those things we had to do; it was part of the war. It was, kind of, you know, it was one of those things that sticks with you for a long time – especially if he'd been a good buddy."*
> Vernon Kahl
> C Co., 20th Infantry Regt.

There was some comic relief too, though, amid the carnage. The Japs started dropping propaganda leaflets on us. They were drawings showing a good looking girl, naked as a jaybird, and an officer with his pants down around his ankles having sex with her. The caption said, "This is what is going on back home while you guys are dying." We collected them and sold them to the Navy and Air Corps guys. Some of the guys got as much as $20 for them. I sold some for a couple of bucks apiece.

One of the nightly air raids was by a plane we called Washing Machine Charlie. We called him that because you could hear his motors sounding really weird, like they were out of sync. Other guys called him Piss Call Charlie because he would come flying in around 4:00 or 5:00 in the morning. He'd drop a 100-lb. bomb usually missing everything, and then fly off. We all got out of our holes and started shooting at him, to no avail. I think every island in the Pacific had a Washing Machine Charlie to liven up the night sky.

*

After two weeks of essentially constant fighting, 63rd Infantry relieved 1st Infantry. We were pulled off the perimeter and we thought we were going to sit on the beach and have a good time. They wanted us to get some sun so we could dry out. If you spent any amount of time in the jungle interior, everything, including you, would start to rot from the constant dampness. "You guys have been in combat for four weeks and we're going to give you a little vacation on the beach," they said. But they couldn't just let us sit around, doing nothing. Not the Army. They had us unloading liberty ships for about six weeks. It's like we had temporarily become a port battalion. We unloaded guns, bombs, all sorts of supplies. The only good thing about that detail was that we had a great opportunity to go onto the ships, find the galley, and trade souvenirs for some decent food. The Navy gave us cases of canned turkey, chicken, whatever they had, and we gave them Japanese rifles, helmets, all the stuff we didn't want. Every couple of days they pulled a couple of guys off port duty to go out on patrol up the river. We always took a water-cooled machine gun in case the patrol got pinned down, but at that time we were only providing covering fire.

By the end of July, most of the 6th Infantry Division units had been relieved from any combat duty by the newly arrived 31st Infantry Division. We were still doing port duty and some patrolling when the scuttlebutt started that we were going to be used as an assault division again somewhere up the coast. It wasn't long before the official word came down from Battalion headquarters. We were moving out. They told us we were going up close to a big Jap naval base farther up the coast. Everyone was trying to figure out where. We didn't have any maps of anything other than the individual areas where we were. Everyone was asking,

"Where the hell are we going? Where is this big Jap base?" It didn't sound too appealing.

> *"The day before we left Maffin Bay, General Robert Eichelberger flew up. We all lined up on the beach for inspection. He walked down the line, pausing to talk to a few guys. He stopped at the fellow right next to me.*
>
> *'Are you scared,' Eichelberger asked.*
>
> *'Yes, I'm scared,' answered the GI.*
>
> *'Well, don't worry about it. We have reconnoitered the area and we're sure there won't be any opposition.' Then he moved down the line.*
>
> *"It was quite impressive to have a three star general standing right next to you. But I was still scared."*
>
> *Mark Bradigan*
> *H Co., 1st Infantry Regt.*

Right before we got ready to make a big push or leave for another beachhead, the quartermaster corps came by with fresh clothing. It was all washed and clean. We took off the clothes we were wearing – some of it was so dirty and sweated up it would practically stand up by itself – dumped it in a big pile and looked through the pile they brought for clothes that were in your size. You just rolled up whatever you weren't wearing and put it in your pack. I knew how disgusting my fatigues had gotten got, so I took an extra pair.

Some of the battalions that attacked Lone Tree Hill had been pretty hard hit, taking lots of casualties. My platoon had been lucky. We had lost a couple of guys to rifle and mortar fire, but we were pretty much intact as the Maffin Bay campaign drew to a close. The regiment had been bloodied and we were now a combat-hardened outfit.

Elsewhere in the Pacific Theater

While the 6th Infantry Division was securing the Maffin Bay area, the Marines continued pushing the Japanese defensive perimeter back in the Central Pacific, invading Saipan in the Mariana Islands, followed by Guam and Tinian. During the Marianas campaign, the U.S. Navy destroyed a significant Japanese carrier force along with perhaps up to 600 naval and ground-based aircraft in the Battle of the Philippine Sea, also known as the Great Marianas Turkey Shoot because of the relative ease with which the Americans shot down Japanese planes.

5. Securing the Bird's Head

Once word came that we were moving out, the rumors started flying. We're going to land here, or we're going to land there. Finally they did tell us. We were landing farther up the coast in an area they called Sansapor-Mar. Well, that was nice, but none of us lowly enlisted men knew where Sansapor-Mar was. I figured we'd find out soon enough.

Right away ordinance came around and started inspecting all our weapons, replacing any that were damaged or defective. And they had personal inspection to see if you had all your gear. Everyone had lost something, but it seemed like just about all of us had managed to lose our gas masks. We figured early on that those were pretty useless, so we simply tossed them away or conveniently forgot them somewhere.

So the Army issued us brand new ones for the landing. They also issued us jungle suits which they said was the latest in tropical combat wear. The jungle suit was a one-piece camouflage suit. But the big problem with them was that they were soaked in some sort of insect repellant in an attempt to keep the malaria-carrying mosquitoes off you. The damned suits wouldn't breathe and we soon had guys dropping from heat exhaustion. Even if you opened them up, it didn't help much. There still wasn't enough air circulation and it was just like wearing a hot suit.

While we were rehearsing for the landing, we actually had a little spare time. The beach where we were had waves, just big enough to horse around in. Some of the guys took their mattress covers, held them up to the wind to fill them with air, then closed them up. They used them to surf the waves. They lasted a couple of runs before they had to fill them up again. So the guys had found a pleasurable use for those mattress covers in addition to their other gruesome use.

When word came to load up, it was in a hurry. One day a bunch of LSTs (Landing Ship Tank) pulled up and they told us to load up. Anything that wasn't consigned or ready to go was to be left on the beach. H Company had a lot of equipment that was still covered with mud and we just left it there on the beach. They needed to get men up to Sansapor-Mar right now and there was to be no more waiting.

The officers told us that the landing area was only 70 miles east of a big Jap naval base at Sorong and west of another Japanese base at Manokwari, and that we should be prepared for a rough beachhead. Sorong was one of their main supply bases for the Southwest Pacific and it was a submarine refueling and refitting base. That made us really nervous because we figured the Japs wouldn't want us landing that close to a major base. They told us the reason we needed to take this area was to establish another forward air base. We were bombing Celebes and the Admiralty Islands at that time and the B24s of the 13th Air Force, coming over from Australia, needed a place to gas up. They came over from Australia, dumped their bombs onto Celebes and Halmahera up there. Then they would come back, gas up, and get out the same day. Since the planes were coming from Australia, I figured they would be good for trade goods and souvenirs. They would have fresh meat and maybe whiskey to trade.

We had aerial pictures of the landing areas and we saw tons of Japanese equipment all over the place. What was surprising, though, was that we didn't see any personnel or native laborers in the pictures. Well, we thought, maybe they headed for cover when they heard the planes coming over.

By 1944 MacArthur's staff had decided on a strategy of leapfrogging the Japanese installations and defenses along the coast of New Guinea and the islands in the Southwest Pacific. Rather than attacking each one that was in his way, he concentrated his limited resources on designated key Japanese positions, isolating others and leaving them to "wither on the vine." This turned out to be a brilliant strategy that reduced the number of casualties his forces would suffer while still achieving his objectives. The decision to seize Sansapor-Mar was part of this strategy, positioning a major Allied force between what would then become isolated Japanese bases at Sorong and Manokwari, while providing him with a major airfield for bombing and support operations. The biggest "non-target" of this strategy was the major Japanese base at Rabaul on the tip of the island of New Britain, with 60,000 troops, 350 miles of tunnels and defenses, and a number of airfields. Rabaul was bombed continuously, and the allied leapfrogging strategy isolated it, rendering it essentially useless to the Japanese war effort. American soldiers never had to invade it.

We left Maffin Bay in the early afternoon and arrived at Sansapor the next morning. We were maybe a mile out at daybreak. The first waves of the 1st Infantry units landed in LCVs (Landing Craft Vehicle) and the latter waves landed in LCIs (Landing Craft Infantry). The LCVs were small wooden boats for landing infantry. The LCIs were the larger craft. I went in on a latter wave in an LCI. They dropped the ramp in a couple of feet of water and we splashed out onto the beach. We were prepared for the worst, but it turned out to be a pushover. We were relieved to find that there was hardly any resistance. We landed just east of the Wewe River near the area called Mar, and by midday we had moved well off the beach. As we spread out from the beach we came across three Japs who were taking notes on the landing. We killed them,

but we didn't know if they had relayed any information back
to their people.

> "I was in a medical clearing company. At
> Sansapor I had a friend who had been inducted at the
> same time as me. That first night I saw him coming
> to our clearing place around 6:30 as a patient. I spoke
> briefly to him but told him that I couldn't spend any
> more time with him because I was scheduled to go on
> guard duty at 7:00.
>
> "There were three of us in a foxhole,
> alternating our watch every two hours. Around 8:00
> I heard someone in the clearing area screaming, "The
> Japs are breaking through." The guy on guard said it
> was one of the patients.
>
> "The next morning I went to see how my
> friend was doing. He was being pronounced dead. I
> think he was the one who was screaming. I heard that
> he had died of a heart attack."
>
> Leo Hennigan
> D Co., 6th Medical Bn.

Sansapor-Mar was on the Vogelkop Peninsula on the
far northwest corner of New Guinea. The name refers to the
shape of the landmass, which vaguely resembles that of a
bird's head, or vogelkop in Dutch. There was a big native
village not very far from the landing beaches. The Japs had
been using them as laborers. This was still Dutch New
Guinea, and we had a couple of Dutch missionaries with us
who could speak the native language. They helped us with
the natives who were only too happy to see us. They were
fuzzy wuzzies similar to the natives we had at Maffin Bay.
They liked to dye their hair a reddish color using the roots of
some tree. I think their life expectancy was about 30 years. If
disease didn't get them, the heat would. They looked old
when they were still young.

As we moved inland we noticed that this area had very few palm trees, but it was covered with tall Kunai grass. The grass was about an inch wide, grew to a height of six to eight feet and had leaves with sharp edges. We would soon learn that the Kunai grass held an enemy just as deadly as the Japs.

The Navy had, as usual, pounded the landing areas and we found a lot of Japs killed by the bombing. But there weren't any natives at the landing area itself, nothing. Everyone was just...gone. We started getting some counterattacks on about the third night, and there was the usual sniper fire here and there, but other than that, and the sporadic air strikes, that was it. We thought we had a real cakewalk.

Then on about the tenth day the first GIs started coming down sick with symptoms that were similar to malaria. The doctors thought at first that it was some different strain of the potentially deadly disease that we knew was a problem throughout the tropics. The guys were suffering with fevers as high as 104 or 105 degrees and they got the shakes. The docs tried to treat it with quinine, the usual treatment for malaria, but it wasn't having any effect. When the guys got up to 106 degrees, they started dying. Eventually the docs figured out that the troops didn't have malaria at all. They were coming down with scrub typhus. We found out from the natives and the Dutch missionaries that the carrier was a mite that lived in that Kunai grass. That's why there had been no one on the beach. The Japs, everyone, had cleared out because of the scrub typhus. The mite would bite you on the soft part of your fingers, or your armpit, or crotch. Then you would get the fever and you'd get a boil that swelled up. That's how you knew you had typhus.

It was an epidemic. I think we had around 700 cases in 1st Infantry and about 1800 cases in the 6th Division. It hit mostly guys on the beach who were still in and near the

Kunai grass. The guys in the front lines were pretty much unaffected because we had moved inland off the beach so quickly. One of my buddies, Irv Cohen, came down with it. He was our company clerk and he had been behind, on the beach at Battalion headquarters. They shipped him off to the hospital and we didn't see him again until almost the end of the war.

We brought in a diesel tanker and just sprayed the whole area with diesel oil. They used diesel rather than gasoline because it would burn rather than explode. They lit the oil and just burned it all up, from the beach right on into the jungle. After that, we had very few new cases of scrub typhus.

Once the beach was established, we went about our normal business of sending out patrols – finding the Japanese and killing them. We didn't get much organized resistance at Sansapor, I guess at least partially due to the typhus. Occasionally we came across a Jap who was just lying there, suffering from typhus, and we would put him out of his misery.

> *"Every patrol that went out, I was assigned. The old timers would say, "You have to face the elephant." I believe that was a Civil War saying for being shot at. I faced the 'elephant' and let me tell you -- Randolph Scott, John Wayne, and Errol Flynn lied. Those Japs could shoot. They pinned me down a couple of times."*
> Milton Galke
> E Co., 1st Infantry Regt.

At Sansapor we lived in foxholes. Usually we had personal holes on either side and behind the machine gun hole. When digging in for the night our procedure was to dig a semicircular hole for the machine gun and set it up, then dig our personal holes. They were close enough so you could roll from one to the other. We had this one big guy in the squad, Grisanti. He must have been six foot five. He always had a hell of a time digging his hole because he was so big. He'd look across to this little guy, I forget his name, and he'd say, "Look at him, he's done already. It ain't fair!"

We took turns standing watch at night, and woe be it for the man who fell asleep on his watch. We stood 90-minute watches on Sansapor. There is nothing quite like it – pitch black, usually raining, often so quiet you could hear a pin drop.

You ate in your foxhole, you fought in it, you slept in it, and you even did your bodily business in it. You don't want to get out of your hole, especially at night to do your business. It could be the last thing you ever did. But when you've got to go, you've got to go. And your trusty helmet, in addition to protecting your head from dangerous flying objects, served as your main toilet facility. You took a leak in it, and, yes you even took a crap in it. Guys would often slide or roll over to the machine gun hole for their nature calls because it tended to be deeper than the personal holes. To take a crap you took some dirt, put it in the bottom, and did your business. Then in the morning you dumped it out and washed it out as best you could. If you were near a kitchen you could wash the helmet out with soapy water from the mess rinse. If not there was usually a creek or stream nearby and you did the best you could.

If it was raining, which it usually was, we put our helmets out on the edge of our foxholes to collect the rainwater. Then you could at least wash your face and maybe shave. One night one of the guys, Olsen, a big guy, had to take a leak. But there were a couple of helmets out and he forgot which one was his. He took the one he thought might be his, did his business, and put the helmet back out there. He didn't want to dump it out because he was afraid the contents would run back down into his hole. So he just left it there. It continued to rain and the helmet pretty well filled up with rainwater.

We got up the next morning and everyone grabbed their helmets and started shaving. Odell Adams, a real religious guy from the south who never swore and was sometimes a little reluctant to pull the trigger during counterattacks, took one look at his helmet and said, "Boy, now I know this place is hell. It even rains piss."

Olsen looked over and knew immediately what had happened. He just broke out in hysterical laughter. He said, "Oh, I must have pissed in the wrong helmet last night."

Adams, however, didn't see the humor of it. He flew at Olsen and we had to pull him off of him. He used a few words that we never heard him say before...or after.

Olsen was sort of a nut. When we got our beer rations he would come around and ask me to sell him my beer. It was GI beer. You had to drink a gallon of it to get a buzz. I told Olsen I'd give him my beer if he would dig my next slit trench. So we had an ongoing deal.

> *"Sanitation was always a concern. Poor sanitation leads to disease, and disease can kill an army just as sure as bullets. If we were in a non-combat area for several days, pits were dug and portable latrines put over them. They were 8-10 holers, double row, back to back. These would serve one or two companies. I think they were filled in after use. If you were going to be in a location for only a few days, a trench about 20 feet long, 12 inches deep, and 8-10 inches wide was dug. You squatted astride this, looking at the guy ahead of you, or where one had been. As the contents filled up, the 'latrine orderly' shoveled the dirt that had been removed back in to cover it up. You were responsible for your own paper, which was a component in your rations. We also kept some inside the webbing or our helmets. The most*

desirable way to answer the call of nature was to take your own shovel, go outside the perimeter, dig your own hole and cover it up afterward. If you saw fresh dirt disturbed you treated it as carefully as if it were a land mine. If you had to go at night, you used your helmet and notified the guys left and right of you if you would be tossing the contents. Otherwise they might open fire at the disturbance."
    C. B. Griggs
    K Co., 1st Infantry Regt.

When we weren't in combat I was doing some trading with the Air Force guys. I brought them Jap equipment and souvenirs and traded them for money, or food, or whiskey. The Air Force wanted souvenirs so badly I was even giving them Jap Arisaka rifles. We hadn't been picking them up for a while because there were so many of them lying around. It was just a matter of getting volunteers to go out on patrols to get souvenirs.

Fresh food was so scarce that we even went out wild boar hunting. The wild boar in the area could get up to four, five, six hundred pounds. We went out a couple of times and then finally got one. It was about four hundred pounds. We lugged it back to camp and Louden, a guy from some place in Arkansas, butchered it. He cut it into chunks and we gave it to the mess cook. He cooked it up and we all ate it. Someone said that we shouldn't have eaten it because it could have been contaminated with some sort of worm. But we didn't care. It was fresh meat, and anyway it was cooked.

One of the guys even tried cooking a parrot once. He shot it out of a tree and tried to stew it in his helmet. He thought it would taste like chicken, but it tasted pretty bad, nothing like chicken.

When we weren't in combat, believe it or not a lot of the guys were making things, artsy-craftsy things. We got our pay in the currency of wherever we happened to be at the time. Since we had come from the British section everyone had these coins, a little bigger than a quarter made out of silver. It was called two bobs. The guys found out that you could take your mess kit spoon and just keep pounding on these coins to make it nice and round for a ring. About the only other thing to do when you weren't patrolling was to go out souvenir hunting for items we could trade for food, or set up a little home brewing.

> "I thought it would be fun to make an airplane out of different sizes of ammunition. I had to find different sizes that would work together. It took me a long time just to gather the ammunition. After I took the cap off a Jap 31, it just slipped into the fuse in the cap of the 75mm that was used for the base. I cut the casing off the shell of the 75mm and used that for the wings and tail of the plane. All I had to work with was a broken hacksaw blade and a fingernail file."
> *Vernon Kahl*
> *C Co., 20th Infantry Regt.*

Being primarily a Southern outfit, no matter where we went, the guys continued to apply their considerable knowledge of home brewing techniques. They claimed that they didn't have the right ingredients, but they always seemed to come up with some semblance of alcoholic beverage. Back home they made it out of corn. At Milne Bay they made it out of raisins. At Sansapor they made it mostly out of apricots, or whatever other dried fruit showed up in our rations.

I succumbed to tasting some at Sansapor. That stuff was 180 proof and they didn't realize it. "My God," I said. "That stuff will clean your teeth and burn off anything that's on them."

Another alcoholic drink was made from medical alcohol. It came in five-gallon cans with wood wrapping around the sides so it wouldn't get damaged. After we found out that you could actually drink the stuff, they guys either tried to steal some or traded with the medics for souvenirs. It was 180 proof too, though, and it burned your mouth if you drank it straight. So they diluted it. And they mixed it with a powdered synthetic lemon juice to give it some flavor. They diluted it down to about 100 proof and had a high old time.

On patrol in Dutch New Guinea, and Sansapor in particular, we saw a lot of crocodiles. In the water they looked like old sunken logs...until they started to move. We used to break open cans of bully beef and toss it to them to eat. Once, one of the guys came up with the bright idea of taking a concussion grenade and sticking it in the beef. The next time we came across a croc, he tossed the lethal package to the croc. It blew up in the water, and all his little croc buddies came in for the feast.

The swamps had another nasty creature...leeches. I never knew what leeches were until New Guinea. Disgusting little creatures. They latch onto you as you go through the swampy water and they suck your blood until they have had their fill. You can't pull them off because their suckers got stuck in you and got infected. You had to touch them with a lit cigarette and that would make them fall off.

One thing we learned on New Guinea was that the Japanese usually dug their foxholes straight down, then after about three feet they would dig horizontally. This helped them survive grenade attacks. We'd throw a grenade into the hole, and thinking we had killed anyone in the hole, we'd move on. Then the Japs would jump up and shoot you in the back. So we started throwing white phosphorus grenades – we called them Willy Petes – into the holes. The white phosphorus burned off all the oxygen and they either died right there in the hole, or they came climbing out for us to pick off.

The Army designated Sansapor cleared up and we finally started setting up tents. Up to that point we had been living in foxholes. To support the tents you needed to have sticks to put through loopholes in the canvas. Some of the local natives hung around camp and helped out with odd jobs. Since we were in Dutch New Guinea we got our pay in Dutch money. We gave the natives some Dutch money for helping out, but what they really wanted were commodities.

One day our duffle bags showed up. We hadn't seen them since we left the States. When we were assigned to the 6th Infantry Division they were all dumped into the 6th Infantry Division supply depot. They started passing them out, and there mine was. But it had ragged holes in it and when I opened it up I found pieces of shrapnel in it. Most of the contents were OK, though.

And there in the duffle was that big old overcoat that I had thrown in there. It was all mildewed and smelled awful. I didn't know what to do with it. I saw one of the natives and called him over. He understood some English so I showed him the coat. He instantly fell in love with that coat, especially those big brass buttons. I told him it was a very valuable coat and had belonged to a general.

"I make you a general, like MacArthur," I said, and I took the coat and put it on him. Here it is all mildewed and still damp, and it's like 120 degrees. But I buttoned it up for him. He was so small and the coat was so big that it reached down almost to his toes. One of the other guys put a helmet on him. The native puffed out his chest and started walking around like he was the man in control. "You general in charge," I told him. "Get your men, cut some good sticks and set up these four tents." It was the funniest thing to see, but no one had any film for their cameras, so we couldn't take a picture.

So I got him and his "men" to set up the tents for all four squads. The guys were laughing. "You got him to do that for the coat?" they asked.

"Yeah," I said. "For the coat. And you guys are going to have to pay for it if the Army charges me for it."

He wore that coat every day. I don't know how he could wear it. I tried telling him to wash it to at least get the mildew out of it, but he didn't appear to understand...or care. When everything was all set up, he disappeared back into the jungle. We never saw him again.

As the camp was expanding, we ran up against some big trees. They were soft wood, but had tremendous root systems. At first we tried to wrap explosive primer cord around the trees to blow them down. That worked, but not well enough for the Army. So they brought in a couple of big bulldozers to dig them up and push them down.

One day this construction guy was sitting in his bulldozer pushing down a bunch of trees. All sorts of foliage was falling around him. On New Guinea the cabs weren't armored; they were just open cabs with canvas tops. That day he happened to knock a huge 17-foot python out of one of the trees and it fell right onto the cab of the bulldozer. The guy was so scared he screamed and jumped off the bulldozer. But he didn't turn it off. He just jumped off and ran. The bulldozer kept on going until it butted up against another tree.

The snake just lay there for a minute and then everyone started shooting at it. They shot it pretty well full of holes. Then the natives came up and chopped it up before carrying it off. I guess it was a delicacy for them. One of them held up a big chunk and said, "For food." We didn't want the thing and we let them have all they wanted.

*

In addition to the usual patrolling we had a special long-range patrol. We went down the coast about 20 or 30 miles toward Sorong. The original plan was to transport us up to our positions on submarines or one of the landing craft.

But the Japs had light destroyers patrolling the area. We could always tell when they were out there because you could hear them in the distance. So we used the PT boats. The boats came in really quickly, in and out. The PT boats took us in and we manned our position for five days. On the fifth day they returned and picked us up. They came in the morning at the designated time, and if you weren't there, they came back one more time in the evening. If you didn't connect, they figured that you weren't coming back.

We had the squad, six guys with machine guns. On the beach where we were going to be dug in we each fired a belt of ammunition to make sure the guns were firing properly. If it jammed we cleared them and were ready to go. A machine gun could jam for several reasons. One was if you changed the barrel and you didn't put the correct head space on it. When you put the new barrel on you tightened it and then clicked it back a few times. If you didn't check the setting you ran the risk of the gun jamming. The guns fired at about 500 – 600 rounds a minute and someone came up with the bright idea of taking the back plate off, unscrewing the buffer section and putting a coin in there. It was supposed to make the gun fire faster. I'm not sure that really did anything, though, except increase the chance of a malfunction. I never used it in combat.

These were "ambushes" set up to get Japanese attempting to travel around the U.S. positions, coming from Wewak or Manokwari, moving up the coast on the beach at night, and sleeping in jungle during the day. They were trying to get to the Japanese base at Sorong. There, they hoped to be evacuated by a Jap sub. By this time the base had been destroyed, but they Japanese who were working their way through the jungle didn't know it.

We just sat there in the jungle along one of the trails the Japs were using to move along the coast, and we would wait. We didn't use walkie-talkies because those were two-way radios and the Japs could pick up the transmissions. For communication we used wired units called sound powers. We had three guys in the rear, and three guys in the foxhole, watching. In the morning we picked up the sound power and sort of whistled into it. If you didn't get a return whistle you knew something was wrong and you were very careful getting out of the hole.

We did one five-day tour and then another squad would come up. We heard from the guys that had gone up previously that you just sit in the jungle and more than likely nothing happens. And that's what happened on our first patrol...nothing.

Most of the Japs coming through looked pretty bad, torn uniforms, poorly armed, half starved. They had been fighting on the island since the drive to take Port Moresby in 1942 and they were spent.

On one patrol a couple of scraggly, half-dead Jap privates did come through on our watch. We figured we wouldn't get anything for capturing those guys, so we let them pass. On another patrol we caught a group of Orientals coming down the trail. A few of them looked like soldiers, but most didn't. They were just walking along carrying their rice like they didn't have a care in the world. Something happened and we opened up on them, killing them all. When we examined the bodies we found that all but a couple of them were non-Japanese, most likely Formosan laborers.

One day at camp the company commander had a wild idea to dig a well to supplement our fresh water supply. One of the southern boys said he could witch for water. He went into the jungle and came back with a stick. He walked around for a while, then stopped and pointed to a spot not far from the battalion CP. A couple of guys volunteered to dig. They got down to about seven or eight feet and smelled gas. Johnson, not thinking, paused and lit a cigarette. The resulting explosion burned his clothes and his chest. The two other guys in the

well weren't hurt but their clothes were burnt. A couple of
other guys took over and they did find water a couple of feet
further down. We took a sample to the hospital to be tested
and it checked out OK. It was pretty good water.

Sometime in October, word came down from
Battalion that a new special group was forming called the
Alamo Scouts. Each company was asked to furnish at least
four volunteers. Noncommissioned officers would get some
sort of special rank. I thought maybe I would give that a try. I
wrote my father about it, saying only that I might be
changing outfits. There would be two months of intensive
training. The plan was to join up with some local guerillas
before our next landing. It would be very dangerous because
we would be behind enemy lines.

I was giving it some serious thought, but by the time I
decided to go for it, they had enough volunteers. In H
Company two guys from mortars and two guys from
machine guns joined the Scouts. We never saw them again.
Maybe they got killed, maybe they got captured, or maybe
they just went different places. Later I heard that the training
included parachute jumps. I thought, no I don't think that
sounds too good. I've never parachuted and I'm not going to
start now. Maybe it was a good thing I was too late.

*

Although I never got typhus, I did get malaria. Since
quinine was in short supply, the Army gave us Atabrine,
which was also effective against the disease. Quinine was
better, but the Japanese had cut off the supply from Java. The
first Atabrine pills didn't have a coating on them and they
were so bitter that a lot of guys flatly refused to take them.
Water was scarce. If you got them in your mouth and there
wasn't enough water to wash them down, which often was
the case, you had to suffer with that awful taste a long, long

time. Eventually they started issuing coated ones that were a lot easier to swallow.

> *"Sometimes we were lined up, given a pill, and an officer watched you take it. After about a week on the stuff you started turning yellow. If you weren't turning yellow, they knew that you weren't taking your Atabrine."*
> C. B. Griggs
> K Co., 1st Infantry Regt.

You had to take the damned things every day, and sometimes we ran out. The docs told us to watch out for the anopheles mosquito. That was the one that carried malaria. Supposedly they come in on you a little differently than other mosquitoes. When they come in on you his head is down and his ass is in the air. Actually only the female feeds on blood. So what, I thought. You never see the damn things anyway until it's too late.

Well I ran out of Atabrine. It was so damned hot and muggy there, and the sun beat down on you. Sometimes our heads felt like they were cooking under our helmets and we took them off if we were in a relatively safe area, even though you risked a nice case of sunburn. And we used to take our shirts off, even though the mosquitoes were like dive bombers. I don't think I ever saw the little bugger that got me. We had been on patrol and I was sitting in the slit trench swatting them away. After we got back to camp I started getting the shakes. I figured, what is this? The medic asked me if I had any quinine pills. I had four tablets, which everyone got. He told me to start taking them and he'd try to find me some more.

"Where have you been?" he asked me.

"We were in the jungle, in the swamps. We ran across a native village back there that appeared to have been evacuated due to disease of some sort."

"Great," he said. "You've got malaria. But I think you're still healthy enough to carry on, even though you feel like you're freezing."

The guys said I had a trip ticket back to the states – some guys with malaria had gotten shipped back – but I told them I didn't think so. I was right. The doctors said, no, "You should go back where you came from," meaning combat.

So there I was, walking around with a blanket around me trying to keep warm, and it was probably 120 degrees in the shade. It lasted about eight or nine days and finally started to dissipate. I thought I was completely cured – I didn't even have to go to the hospital – but I suffered a few more attacks later on.

After I recovered I went out on a couple of more long-range patrols. Nothing much had happened on any of mine and I thought my next one would be another five or six days to goof off, and maybe capture some prisoners. But this time was to be different.

This was a bigger patrol, about 30 guys. The PT boat sped us up the coast and dropped us off. Some of the guys stayed on the beach and the rest of us hiked over to our assigned position. We traded off going up into the jungle. We had been there a couple of days and it was my turn to go. We set up the machine gun and the riflemen from E Company were supposed to have secured the area. We dug our foxholes like little pillboxes, spread out over the area. The night was uneventful. When I got up in the morning I whistled into the sound power. Two riflemen and I were due to relieve the forward men. There wasn't any return whistle, so I whistled again. No response.

I threw down the sound power. Ah, those dumb bastards are out of their hole. Probably both taking a leak. I looked around and didn't see anything. So I got out of my hole and followed the wire through the thick jungle foliage. It led to a dugout that made use of part of a downed coconut log for reinforcement. Actually it had the looks of an old Jap dugout. It was a good location overlooking a little stream close to a path that the Japs were using to evacuate from Manokwari.

The two riflemen trailed behind me. I wanted to get close enough to whisper to the men in the dugout not to shoot. We didn't do any shooting up there unless we had to because we didn't want to tip the Japs off to where we were. We did have a couple of patrols that got wiped out, most likely because they started shooting. When that happened we had to abandon that area and find another one further up or down the beach. These long-range patrols, in fact most of the Sansapor engagement, were a cat and mouse sort of thing. I crept closer cautiously. Still no response. When I reached the entrance, I peered into the hole.

I recoiled in horror. They were both dead. Their throats had been cut. Although I knew I shouldn't, I couldn't resist the driving urge to get out of there...fast. I scampered out of the hole. As soon as I got out I heard the rat-a-tat from a Nambu, a Japanese machine gun, and I heard the bullets hitting the ground. One hit my leg, grazing the flesh.

I kept running after I was hit and dove for cover. Meanwhile the riflemen cut the sniper out of the tree where he had been hiding. If he was the guy that killed our buddies, then good riddance to him. It wasn't a bad wound, but our position had been compromised, and we had to head back down to the beach where the rest of the patrol was, including the medic. We carried our men out with us. Back on the beach the medic looked over my wound, put a dressing on it and bandaged it.

The next morning the PT boat came, as scheduled, to pick us up. I ran, gimpy leg and all, out to that boat. All of us did. We wanted out of there as quickly as possible. We had a full contingent of guys to get on that PT boat, and we were carrying our two comrades. The Navy guys were usually pretty cocky, but they quickly got silent and solemn when they saw the two bodies wrapped in their ponchos.

Back at Sansapor, things had settled into a pattern. I kept to myself a bit. I was always sort of separate from the rest of the guys because I was Jewish and there were only a few Jews in the company. Rosenthal was Jewish and so was Irv Cohen our company clerk. I had a little folding camera my father had given me before I went overseas and he gave me a half dozen rolls of 120 film. I had to be pretty judicious with my picture taking because once that film was gone there most likely wouldn't be any more. The Army would develop your film for nothing but it was pretty heavily censored. I made a deal with the Air Corps for some developing and I developed the film myself in a little darkroom set up in a tent.

I actually had a pretty good thing at Sansapor. We had captured lots of Jap rifles, helmets, mess kits, and other stuff, and I was taking them down to the Air Corps and trading for food. The Air Corps had the good food down at the airstrip where they serviced the planes. They flew it in from Australia. They asked if I could get Jap helmets, and I told them I could get all they wanted, plus rifles, "All you want." One guy asked me if I could get a Japanese head, but I told him, "No, I only deal in merchandise." So I was down there all the time, trading Japanese souvenirs for food, mostly cases of canned goods. I loaded up a jeep with souvenirs and brought back some pretty good grub.

One time Wheeler, our company commander, saw me coming back with a jeep full of canned food. "How'd you get that?" He pointed to the food.

"Well, I took one of the jeeps…"

"You took a jeep?"

"Yes, it was just sitting there at the motor pool." The airstrip was about three miles down the road from camp. The motor pool guys always let me take a jeep because I would give them some of the food.

He thought for a moment and then said, "OK, see if you can get some whiskey next time." I gave him some whiskey, but it didn't seem to do me any good.

Wheeler didn't like me, or anyone else for that matter, except maybe his fellow officers. That was fine. None of us liked him either. I was supposed to get promoted to sergeant at Sansapor – I had been doing the job for a while since our platoon sergeant got wounded – but Wheeler didn't want to give me the promotion because I would be getting some additional pay for it. It wasn't that much, really. In addition to the rank pay we got $5.00 a month for the expert infantry badge, $10.00 for the combat infantry badge, and $5.00 for each medal you got.

Mark Bradigan saw me coming back from one of my runs one day with a couple bottles of whiskey. He asked me to give him some, but I told him, no, it was for sale because one way or another I had to pay for it. He asked how much I wanted for it and I told him $50.00. He scraped the money together and I sold him a bottle, but he always thought that I should have given him one.

"Although we were in the same platoon, I really didn't know Leonard until we hit Sansapor. We were different guys. During down time, I played a lot of softball and football. Leonard spent most of his time taking pictures. I was amazed that he found a way to get them developed. But he was quite a wheeler dealer. He did a lot of trading with the Air Corps guys from the nearby base.

"I was only 19 but I had quite a taste for whiskey and Leonard said he could get a bottle of Canadian whiskey for $50.00. I had most of the money but had to borrow the rest. The deal was that Leonard would get one drink from the bottle.

"I really wanted that whiskey. I don't think we had any alcoholics in the unit, but there were a lot of guys who really loved their whiskey. Some were mixing Bay Rum with rubbing alcohol and powdered lemonade and drinking that. They got high, alright, but they got whacky too. Other guys tried to brew their own stuff from prunes they got from the kitchen. It was all pretty awful.

"I bought the bottle and let Leonard have his drink. Then six or eight of us got together behind a tent. We took a swig and passed the bottle. It didn't last too long, but it sure was good."

Mark Bradigan
H Co., 1st Infantry Regt.

Mail call was a very important event. It was our only link with home. When we were in combat we got mail once a week if we weren't under heavy fire. Usually the letters were happy ones, from wives and sweethearts or family members. Sometimes the women would put perfume on the pages. We'd gather around the lucky guy and take in a good whiff. Occasionally one of the guys would get a "dear John" letter. You could always tell. You saw it in their faces. The letters were usually along the same lines. The wife or the girlfriend had left him. She saw no reason to wait because there was a chance that he wasn't coming back. It was so sad to see the look on the poor guys face. Here he was fighting for his life, and his girl gets tired of waiting, or finds someone else, and says good-bye. I tried to understand it, but I never could.

Packages usually made their way to us, eventually, and a lot of guys got food items. Sometimes they offered to share, sometimes not. Whenever I got something I offered to share it with the guys. The packages often included candy bars, real ones, but after being transported in the ships' holds they would melt into one big mess. My father wrote me pretty regularly, and I wrote him too. One time he traded his food stamps and got me a salami. He stuck it inside a cardboard tube from some wrapping paper and shipped it. I'll never forget when it arrived. The mail clerk came and he was dragging his mailbag behind him. Usually he carried it over his shoulders. He said someone had shipped something that died on the way over. The package had my name on it. I unwrapped it and there was the salami... totally rotten. I offered to share it, but surprisingly no one took me up on it. I got rid of that rotten thing pretty quickly. I threw it in a foxhole that we were filling in.

Since we were near an air base, there were plenty of damaged, spare and used parts around. The Air Corps gave us some air-cooled .30-caliber machine guns that they had taken out of some of the planes because they didn't pack enough punch against the Japanese planes. They had pistol grips like the .50-cals did. They gave us chests full of ammunition with the guns. We were happy to see all that new ammunition, but we couldn't use it in our existing guns because these were link-fed. Our guns used belt-fed ammunition.

The Air Corps .30-caliber ammunition came in three varieties. Black-tipped was armor piercing, silver-tipped was explosive, and blue-tipped was incendiary. Although we couldn't use it in the machine guns, they guys loaded them into their M1 clips. When you hit a Jap with those rounds, you knew it. Our regular machine gun ammunition usually had one round of red-tipped, which was a tracer, then three rounds of ball, then one round of AP, although the mix could change when they loaded the belts. The ammunition came in bandoliers and if you pulled them out of the chest you could carry it around you. The problem with that was, once you opened the chests the ammunition had to be used. Otherwise it would become mildewed. And when it got wet it could jam the guns. That's why the Army eventually would go to metal clips for some of the guns.

One night I came back to camp from making one of my Air Corps trading runs. I took the jeep back over to the motor pool and was unloading the food I had gotten. As I recall on that run it was cases of canned pineapple. I thought I saw something moving off in the brush. Everything grew so fast out there it was hard to keep the foliage from growing right back up to the edge of camp. Curious, I walked toward where I had seen the movement, which was not a very smart thing to do. The Japs had been infiltrating our lines pretty regularly, stealing food and supplies. Suddenly a Jap popped up and fired a shot at me, and ran off into the night.

I got hit right above the knee. It felt like getting hit with a baseball bat followed by a burning sensation. I had my .45 and I emptied the clip into the brush, then sat down on the ground. I heard the guys in camp saying, "Hey, who's shooting his gun off?"

"I'm hit. I'm hit," I yelled. And by that time there was a small crowd of guys around me. I heard someone say, "You got him, Gordy."

Luckily the bullet didn't hit me at full power. Apparently the guy had run out of oil for his bullets; that was a big problem in New Guinea because of the pervasive moisture. The bullet hit me right where the nerves are so there was very little pain. It was more of a burning sensation, like someone had taken a hot iron and stuck it there. And then it started to bleed.

My first thought was, my God I'm hit. But then I realized that by comparison it wasn't that bad. I wasn't experiencing pain anything like some of the guys who had gotten badly wounded experienced. They were the ones really in pain. This was just a big bloody mess, but not much pain. Since the bullet severed the nerves, I didn't have much feeling in the area, and still don't to this day.

An aid man appeared out of nowhere, as they usually did when someone was hit. Those guys were amazing. No matter what was happening or how hot the action was, they always tried to get to you.

I tried to get up, but he said, "Oh, you're not going to walk anywhere. You're going to the field hospital." He put a pack on it to control the bleeding. "Does it hurt?"

"It burns like hell," I said. They put me on a stretcher, loaded the stretcher on a jeep, and drove me to the field hospital.

This was crazy. I had fought at Maffin Bay, taking a beach under fire and participating in one of the bloodiest battles of the New Guinea campaign at Lone Tree Hill, and I didn't get so much as a scratch. And here at Sansapor, where we mostly went out on patrol looking for the enemy, I get wounded – twice. But a bullet is a bullet and you can get just as dead from a patrol or a sniper as you can from a major assault.

They took me to the 11th Portable Surgical Hospital. The doctors operated on my leg right there in an operating tent. They gave me a spinal, so even though I was laid flat I could see what the docs were doing. I felt them probing around, scraping and cutting, but there wasn't any pain. They said they had to cut a pretty big swath in my leg because the bullet didn't go in cleanly. That was a problem with a lot of Jap bullets. They had a habit of sort of tumbling during flight, even from a well-maintained gun. Well, this one went in, hit the bone, and created a lot of little chips. So they were probing around to make sure they got all the bone chips out. But luckily there wasn't any serious damage to the leg, just a lot of blood. One of the doctors kept saying, "Oh, you've got a good one there. You're going back."

Goldsmith came to see me the next day. I thought maybe he'd finally have a kind word to say to me. I was wrong.

"Don't expect a Purple Heart for this," he said.

"Why not?" I asked.

"We were out of combat," he said. "You're not getting a Purple Heart."

"Bit sir, I was wounded. And I killed a guy."

"You don't know if it was the one you shot. He may have been wounded. And you don't really know what happened."

"They never found his body," I said. "He took off into the jungle."

Goldsmith was unmoved, but the Army thought differently. That was my first Purple Heart.

I was in the field hospital for about three weeks. It was monsoon season and we were still getting sporadic air raids. So anyone who had a leg wound or couldn't walk was housed in a dugout that had a tent over it. During monsoon season, you would have a dull overcast, then the sun would come out, then it would rain for three of four hours. Then the sun would come out again. But then it would rain for three days straight, without stopping. And because of the heavy rains, the hospital dugout was always filling up with water. Half the time the bottom of my cot was soaking wet. A lot of the guys from my platoon came to visit me, and that helped pass the time.

In the hospital most of the patients talked about their home towns and their girlfriends. I didn't have a girlfriend so mostly I talked about what I was doing in Chicago, that my father was a photographer, and the work I was doing for him. Most of the guys were farmers and a lot of them couldn't read or write. They had enlisted in the service so they could get food to eat. I didn't really get too friendly with any of them. The orderlies were mostly conscientious objectors who did not want to fight. Some of them were ashamed about it and they talked about their religion as the reason.

By that time I figured I'd had enough of the jungles, and the rains, and the Japs, and I was hoping I had that million-dollar wound that would send me home. But as I continued to heal at the field hospital, something strange happened. The longer I was there, the more I wanted to get back to my unit, or more accurately, to the guys in the unit. I began to feel like I was letting them down. The doctor came around and said I was fit for limited duty and he was going to send me back. "They need everyone who can walk right now."

"But I got hit in the leg," I said.

"We thought you had a trip ticket back to the states, but we were wrong. Sorry."

I just said, "OK."

I joined some other returning GIs and some replacements and we loaded up on some brand new LCIs that had just arrived. We made a short, uneventful trip back up to Sansapor, stopping at Finschafen for a day to pick up another group of replacements. These guys were green troops, fresh from the States. When we got back to Sansapor, I still had a noticeable limp.

I reported to regimental headquarters. The company commander, Wheeler, said, "Well look, the Jewish goldbrick is back." He said it half jokingly. I wanted to say something back, but I figured I had better just keep my mouth shut. It's probably a good thing that I did, because not long after I returned I was made squad leader. But I didn't get the stripes until we got to the Philippines.

I went through the mess line and sat down next to Red Ellis. I called him Tracer Ellis because when the fighting started he would sometimes high-tail it for the rear and all you would see was his bright red hair streaking by you. I was his squad leader and he was my first gunner. He had shot himself in the hand early on at Sansapor. He said that he was cleaning his .45 automatic, pulled the slide back, and it went off and shot him in the hand. But for someone who was left-handed, his wound was in the wrong hand. The Army suspected it to be a self-inflicted wound, and, after a brief stay in the hospital he was sent back to the unit. He was angry with me because he thought I had reported that he had shot himself intentionally. Well, he was partly right. Most of the guys in the squad had the same notion, but I was the one who had to put it in the report. He was always getting into trouble, though, and before we left Sansapor he was transferred to the quartermaster corps.

I was talking to Ellis when one of the guys from mortars came by, Nusarino. He used to call me Jew Boy or refer to me as a Dirty Jew all the time. He said, "Hey Jew Boy, get your mess kit out of here. I'm taking this spot," and he pushed my mess kit and food away. He was a little bigger than me and I was always a little scared of him. But I was so mad, I figured, the hell with it, let them court-martial me. I picked up that mess kit and I smacked him in the face with it. Then I got him down and started beating the crap out of him.

The other guys all gathered around and they started yelling, "Kill the bastard." Most of the guys didn't like him. I beat the hell out of him pretty badly. But after that we actually became pretty good friends. Sadly, he contracted cerebral malaria later on and died from the disease. I was digging ditches for a week for fighting, bad leg and all. Wheeler said, "That will teach you to pick on somebody."

"Pick on somebody? He threw my food on the ground."

"Couldn't you just go back and get another tray?"

"Nobody calls me a Dirty Jew," I said.

Well, at least I didn't get court-martialed.

By the time I got back to the regiment the division was already preparing for our next beachhead. They didn't tell us where it was to be, but they told us it was going to be the biggest beachhead in the Pacific. Most of the squad was still intact, but we did have a couple of replacements.

The Army had us doing cargo net training – going up and down the cargo nets alongside the transports. Wheeler wanted me to climb the ropes like the rest of the company. "My leg is still draining and they told me to take it easy on it," I said.

He snapped back, "So have the aid man put a bandage on it."

So I went to the doc's and they gave me a light duty slip. That meant that I didn't have to do any cargo nets. That didn't sit too well with Wheeler, but he couldn't do anything about it. He kept growling that I wouldn't be prepared, and he managed to get the light duty slip canceled early.

"When we make the landing you won't be able to climb up and down the ladder."

"My leg will be ruined and it will get infected."

"Doc Mullins will put a bandage on it every day."

"What about my fatigues. The more I move around the more it drains and it's ruining my fatigues." I only had two pairs of fatigues. "I'll have to wash them and change them back and forth, and there's no water for that."

"You can use the slop water, it's not going to hurt anything," and he dismissed me.

So I shuffled my way through the cargo net training for a while. Doc Mullins changed my bandage every day and I used the slop water to wash my fatigues. The joke turned out to be on Wheeler, however, because after we did all this cargo net training, the Navy showed up with LVTs (Landing Vehicle Tracked), also called water buffaloes. These landing craft had tracks like a tank. They are loaded up right on the transport ship and they take you right up onto the beach. So we wouldn't be using the cargo nets. All that training was for nothing and that made Wheeler even angrier.

For about six weeks in November and December we trained for the next beachhead...all sorts of maneuvers...though we still didn't know where we were going. It was monsoon season, real heavy rains, but we did everything right through the rains. Scuttlebutt had us going to Formosa or the Philippines, depending on who you listened to. I was assigned to port battalion a couple of times, loading and unloading boats at the dock, and I was talking to the sailors, merchant marines actually, who were crewing the boats. They told us that down the coast at Hollandia – that's where MacArthur's headquarters were at the time – the Navy was going to assemble the biggest armada of ships they had ever seen in the Pacific. But, scuttlebutt is just scuttlebutt and we waited for news of where we were going.

> *"At Sansapor I was put in the motor pool for a while. It was a cushy job because I didn't have to do any of the training the other guys were doing. I was hauling water from a water filtration station they had set up near this river to the company kitchen. They had made a reservoir and we filled up five-gallon cans and took them to the kitchen. I was driving a ¾-ton truck. The company commander had come out with an order that everyone had to wear shirts and long pants because of the mosquitoes and malaria. It was a really hot day so I took off my shirt. Boy, was I stupid. This guy, Novak, came running up to me. He was the company runner assigned to Battalion HQ and Major Meyers. Meyers was really a stickler. Novak said that Meyers wanted to see me. Major Meyers just ripped me a new one for not wearing a shirt. He said I wasn't following orders. I was sent back to regular duty. So I lost my cushy job."*
> *Mark Bradigan*
> *H Co., 1st Infantry Regt.*

We cleaned and tested all our gear and we practiced loading, unloading, and storming the beach. We continued to get hit by real heavy monsoons, but we continued practicing. In one exercise we loaded up on LSTs and they took us about two miles out. Then we loaded into water buffaloes and circled around until someone fired a flare, which was the signal to turn for the beach. We motored to the beach where they dropped the front ramp. We unloaded and went through the motions of establishing a beachhead.

One day, after we had gotten hit by a typhoon, the rains had let up, but the tides were high and the water was really rough. We loaded up on the water buffaloes about two miles out as usual. But this time the seas were too rough. I saw the back end of some of the boats lift right out of the water. A couple of the water buffaloes overturned on the way to the beach. We were lucky in 2nd Battalion. My boat made it in, although we were all soaking wet from the waves and overspray. We had one water buffalo overturn and several guys got trapped underneath. Fortunately it was near the shore, and we were able to get a bulldozer to it to flip it over. The guys were OK, trapped in an air pocket. One of them was the 1st sergeant from G Company. He had some pretty choice words for the Army when they pulled that boat off him.

Some of the other battalions weren't so lucky. We lost a couple of water buffaloes further out and they couldn't get to them. The guys trapped underneath drowned. I don't know how many guys we lost but each water buffalo had 35 or 40 guys plus the Navy crew. Afterward there was a big investigation. The IG's office, Inspector General, came by to see if we were being taken care of by command because this thing was such a calamity...and a totally avoidable one. There was no reason to take the troops out if it was that rough. Command would never attempt a landing those seas.

Even the LSTs were getting pushed around. For the next two weeks we had search parties going up and down the beach recovering the bodies that washed ashore.

On Thanksgiving we actually got some turkey. It was real turkey, but they had to prepare it on the ships and send it over to us because we didn't have any ovens in camp. It was OK. They served it with cranberries that tasted so sour you could hardly eat them.

After Thanksgiving the training got more intense, morning, noon and night. Then we started getting briefings and we learned that we were headed for somewhere in the Philippines. But they didn't say exactly where. We knew that Leyte had already been invaded, so we figured it would be Luzon. Wheeler told us that with the current plans, we probably wouldn't be fighting as an intact division. For the landing, 6th Infantry Division would be the spearhead to establish the beachhead. Then if everything went according to plan, we would be formed up into RCTs, Regimental Combat Teams. Instead of fighting as a division, each regiment would go off on its own assignment as a self-supported unit. So they started preparing 1st Infantry for our assignment. They didn't tell us any specific locations, but from the type of objective they were talking about, it sounded to us like ours would be Manila.

The preparations continued. We received a bunch of new replacements and all brand new equipment. One morning, around December 18, the quartermaster came around and issued us new clothing, so we knew we were nearing our departure date. We got new gas masks, jungle suits and cans of dubbin, all of which no one wanted. The gas masks were useless, the jungle suits were unbearable and the dubbin waterproofed your boots so the water and sweat that got into them never got out of them. So most of us just buried that stuff in the jungle outside of camp.

Ordinance replaced our machine guns. They adjusted or replaced any weapon that didn't look perfect. They made sure that everyone had more than enough ammunition, not like the Maffin Bay beachhead where we had ordinance problems. Like before, just about any weapon you wanted, you got, so long as you had a weapon.

On December 23 we loaded our gear onto the LSTs. Any ammunition that we couldn't take with us was buried in big pits or dumped into the ocean. We must have buried or sunk tons of old and corroded ammunition. Any trucks and other vehicles that we didn't want to take with us because they were too beat up were driven, or pushed, onto LSTs. The Navy ferried them out into the ocean and pushed them overboard. They took all the old landing craft and lined them up end to end between the two islands off the coast. Then they pulled the plugs and sank them to make an artificial breakwater.

On December 25 we loaded up on the LSTs for the trip to the Philippines. The LSTs were freshly outfitted with big steel pontoons on each side. But when we got onboard we noticed that there weren't any bunks.

"Hey, there's no bunks. Where are we supposed to sleep?" I asked.

"You're going to sleep in your water buffaloes."

Oh, that's great, I thought. Our LST had six water buffaloes on it plus some trucks. Six water buffaloes, one to join each landing wave. I was on the first wave so I was on the first water buffalo.

We got a Christmas meal. Turkey. Oh boy, I thought, a decent Navy meal. I got into the chow line that was set up with two big garbage cans full of water. The first had soapy water, the second was clear, relatively, hot water. You dipped your mess kit into the soapy water, then rinsed it off and got your chow. But to everyone's great disappointment, it wasn't Navy turkey. It was Army turkey, which was a pretty inferior meal.

The assault parties left first. The rear echelon personnel, such as battalion and division headquarters, would be departing a day later and would catch up to us. I can't say I was sorry to see Sansapor fade off into the distance, but at the same time I didn't know what was in store for us in the Philippines. That night we had another turkey dinner, compliments of the Navy.

It was a huge convoy, ships as far as you could see. When we started out it was just a few ships. Then, every day, we looked out in the morning and there were more ships that had joined in the night. Destroyers, cruisers, even a couple of big battlewagons. In addition to the LSTs, I saw LSIs (Landing Ship Infantry) and APAs. At first I thought that maybe we would be going in on LCIs, because they could hold an entire company and cruise right up to the beach. But we were to remain with our LST. These LCIs were outfitted with rockets. It was the first time any of us had seen that. Each LCI had maybe a thousand rockets, each equivalent to an 81mm mortar with a 25- or 30-pound charge. After the sixth wave, the troops would be going in on the APAs.

During transport, every morning we had calisthenics to keep in shape. Then we got an intelligence briefing, but we still didn't have any official word of exactly where we were going. Even after we began to learn about the invasion location, the Army cautioned us not to write anything about the invasion in our letters, because if the ship went down the Japs might pick it up. They said to write that we were going somewhere in the Pacific.

Then we lost our first ship.

A submarine hit one of our APAs. The APA was a couple of miles behind us. We heard the explosions and we could see the flashes because it took a couple of hits. And in a convoy like that you can't stop. You're going at convoy speed, about seven or eight knots, and you can't afford to stop, or even slow down. There are ships in the convoy designated for rescue and recovery.

My ship didn't get hit but we did lose one guy. His name was Farmer. He was leaning over the side and he just lost his balance. As the guys on deck watched him flounder in the water, a destroyer appeared out of nowhere. We learned later that it had picked him up. Other than being wet and thoroughly embarrassed, he was OK.

By about January 3 or 4, the guys were starting to get antsy. It's a long time with no bunks or showers other than the saltwater variety, just enough water for shaving, and one canteen cup of water a day plus whatever they gave you with your meals. We got two meals a day, breakfast and supper.

Security onboard was tight. We weren't allowed on deck after it got dark unless you were on guard duty. We had a rotating guard duty and we manned the antiaircraft guns on the boat alongside the Navy guys. The boat was your little island of life and after a while you got so you knew where just about everything was. You could go down in the hold where the LVTs were. Down there they had red lights, a deep red light that wasn't supposed to affect your night vision. You'd just lie there, or play some cards, read a book, or write a letter. Everything down there picked up this sort of sea mildew odor and after a while everyone got just plain fed up. Nerves became unhinged and fights broke out over the most meaningless things, girls back home, dice, cards, just about anything you could think of.

As we approached the Philippines we started getting Japanese kamikaze plane attacks. They usually came out of the sun so you couldn't see them until they were almost on you. The LST's 40-mm Bofors antiaircraft guns blazed away at them. An APA to the right of us took a direct hit. It just blew up and went right down. As always, we had no choice but to keep on going. Destroyers and destroyer escorts swooped in, their distinctive whoop

whoop whoop horns sounding, and picked up as many survivors as they could.

One kamikaze came in around 06:00 just as it was getting light. It came in right over our heads and it was so low it seemed like you could almost reach right out and touch it. It crashed into the LST next to us, starting a deck fire, but thankfully not doing a lot of damage. The LST had to get rid of its pontoons and the Navy had to sink them because they were airtight and would disrupt the convoy. There were some casualties on the LST, but all things considered, they were pretty lucky.

> *"Several of the planes were turned into flaming wreckage, but one banked into a long dive and headed toward our vessel. Several sailors whose duties required them to remain on deck were hit by flying parts of the disintegrating plane. But our LST was only damaged slightly to its superstructure; we continued to hold our place in the convoy."*
> Robert Damm
> 1st Field Artillery

> *"Now another plane flew just above the water and weaved between the ships. He knew we couldn't fire at him at a low level because we could hit another ship. When the pilot got on the outside where the destroyers were, he took off up in the air. But we saw a puff of smoke, so, I guess he didn't make it."*
> Vernon Kahl
> C Co., 20th Infantry Regt.

Around January 7 they told us if we wanted to write any letters home, now was the time to do it. In the briefings they said that they anticipated that this was going to be a rough beachhead. Command was expecting that casualties could be as high as 50% for the first three or four waves. Regardless of what happened around us, we were to keep moving in. We would be landing on Blue Beach and our objective was to reach the Mangaldan-Dagupan Road. What was funny was that was the first time I had heard anyone mention the word road in any strategic sense. On New Guinea we really didn't have any.

The chow onboard got better too, and that was another signal that we were getting close to our destination. On January 8 they passed out beer and cigars, cigarettes, toothpaste, all sorts of stuff. So I said, "Ah, tomorrow is the big day." The new guys asked me why I was saying that, and I told them that the Army always passed this stuff out the day before a landing. It suddenly dawned on me that to these new guys, especially the young ones, I was a veteran, experienced, hardened by combat. But hell, I wasn't much more than a kid myself.

> *"I came to the U.S. from Mexico as a child in 1918 to escape the Mexican Revolution. I enlisted in the Army at age 33 because I wanted to do something for the country that had given me such great opportunity.*
>
> *"On the transport to Luzon, some of younger guys, especially the new replacements, were crying because they were afraid of going in to battle. They looked up to me because I was older. I tried to set them at ease."*
>
> Gary Mendoza
> A Co., 1st Infantry Regt.

> *"On January 8, the night before the landing, I heard a radio broadcast by Tokyo Rose. She would always talk to the GIs, try to mess with their heads. She said, "Welcome to the 6th Infantry. We have a warm reception planned for you tomorrow." That really scared me."*
>
> Leo Hennigan
> D Co., 6th Medical Bn.

That evening a Protestant chaplain came around. He held services and asked if we had any messages to send home. That scared some of the guys. It was the first time we had seen so much high-profile religion and it left some of the guys with a dead, sickening feeling, like maybe a lot of them wouldn't make it.

We operated under complete radio silence. The ships communicated with each other using light signals. The convoy approached Luzon from the south and made a wide swing around the west side of the island. We wanted the Japs to think that we were going to land on the northern tip of the island, around Baguio. The Navy had been shelling up north for some time and naval aircraft were making sorties around the area. The deception must have worked because the Japs wound up sending their 2nd Armor Division up north. Then we swung the entire convoy around and turned south into Lingayen Gulf. We were going to land on the southern shore of the gulf, right where the Japs had landed in 1941. That probably rankled MacArthur, but strategically it was the best choice.

> The southern shore of Lingayen Gulf, to the northwest of the capital of Manila, offered flat beaches, good invasion terrain. Once established ashore MacArthur's troops would have decent roads and perhaps even railroads to drive down the central plains to the capital city of Manila. The area also provided enough room for his large invasion force to maneuver. Strategically, seizing the Manila area and the central core of the island would make it hard for the defenders to coordinate their activities. That's why the Japanese had landed there in December 1941.

As we were swinging around the west side of Luzon, off to the distance toward shore in the evening sky we saw flashes followed by bright streaks of light leaping skyward.

We learned later that some of the convoy ships were dispatched to deal with some Jap ships that were making a sortie out of Manila Bay and they had sunk them off Mariveles.

The next day we would be landing on Luzon.

Elsewhere in the Pacific Theater

In September, 1944 U.S. forces invaded the islands of Morotai and Peleliu to provide support bases for the coming invasion of the Philippines. Peleliu stands out as perhaps the one invasion that turned out to be not strategically necessary. The fighting was particularly brutal and bloody and the island was never used in the staging of the Philippine invasion.

In October the U.S. began air raids against Okinawa at the southern extreme of the Japanese home islands in preparation for invasion. The bombing campaign would last over four months. Later that month General MacArthur kept his pledge to return to the Philippines as the Sixth Army invaded the island of Leyte. And the U.S. Navy dealt the Japanese another significant naval defeat in the Battle of Leyte Gulf.

As the year drew to a close the U.S. air forces began a three-month bombing campaign against Iwo Jima in preparation for invasion, and U.S. troops landed on Mindoro in the Philippines.

Cover Photo: Leonard,
probably on Luzon, the
Philippines, 1945

Sansapor, New Guinea,
November 1944

Luzon, the Philippines,
February 1945

With Comedian Joe E.
Brown, Luzon, the
Philippines, April 1945

Near Banaue, Luzon, the Philippines, July 1945

Near Baguio, Luzon, the Philippines, August 1945

Too Much to Drink in Korea, October 1945

Home, 1946

6. MacArthur Returns

Early on the morning of January 9 we loaded into our water
buffaloes. My LVT was pretty quiet. Just guys going about
their grim business, preparing to engage the enemy. The
ship's commander said that the Navy was behind us and that
they'd do everything they could to get us onto the beach. If
some of the landing craft didn't make it to the beach, they
would try to pick us up.

It was around 06:00 when we hit the water, about
three miles out. Originally we thought we would be about
two miles out, but Command decided to launch the invasion
further out to be sure that the landing ships would be out of
range of Jap shore batteries. Our first look at the invasion was
an awesome sight. The morning sky was speckled black with
antiaircraft fire. Every ship was firing away. Everyone was
tense; you could see it in our faces. Everyone from the
generals down to the lowest private feared that this was
going to be a tough and bloody beachhead.

We formed up and circled for a while, waiting for the
signal to head to the beach. The Navy was still pounding the
landing area, as they had been doing for the last two days.
The pre-invasion barrage included the battleships Missouri
and North Carolina. Every time they fired those big 16-inch
guns the entire ship rocked and our little LVT was practically
lifted out of the water.

We got the signal and the LVT operators gunned their
motors and turned toward the beach. The first wave was
moving in. The Navy was still firing their big guns and we
heard the shells whirring overhead. Then the rocket-loaded

LCIs moved in. When they got within about a mile of the beach, they fired their load. On every side of us, it looked like ten thousand rockets streaked toward the beach. Man, I thought, how could anything live through this.

As we got closer to the beach, we hunkered down in the LVT. The Navy guys manned the craft's .50-caliber machine guns. But we weren't taking any fire from the beach. Nothing. So we figured that the Japs had abandoned the beach and had moved inland.

We rode up onto Blue Beach around 09:30. An American fighting force had returned to Luzon.

> *Although the U.S. Army had already invaded the southern island of Leyte, the prize of the Philippines strategically and politically was the island of Luzon with its capital, Manila, the Pearl of the Orient. On January 9, 68,000 men of General Walter Kruger's Sixth Army landed on Luzon on the beaches of Lingayen Gulf. Over the next few days a total of 203,600 men came ashore in the largest amphibious invasion of the Pacific theater.*
>
> *The U.S. Army divisions that fought in the Luzon campaign were:*

6th Infantry Division	*38th Infantry Division*
24th Infantry Division	*40th Infantry Division*
25th Infantry Division	*41st Infantry Division*
32nd Infantry Division	*43rd Infantry Division*
33rd Infantry Division	*11th Airborne Division*
37th Infantry Division	*1st Cavalry Division*

They dropped the ramp and we scampered onto the beach. We didn't encounter any Jap fire, so the word was to move in. We were scared that the Japs were waiting for us just off the beach, but for the first hour after landing, we had free reign. As we moved inland the Filipinos were coming out of their bomb shelters, men and boys in shorts and girls in western-style dresses, and they were yelling "Victory, Joe," with smiles as big as their faces. They were so happy to see Americans again. They offered us eggs, bananas, chickens, anything we wanted. At one point we saw some of the big 16-inch shells from the battleships dug partway into the ground. Duds apparently. A lot of those big shells were ammunition left over from World War I. Some little Filipino kids were crawling all over one. We left there in a hurry.

Once off the beach we passed rice paddies, one after another. My machine gun platoon moved again with E Company. There were English-speaking civilians, small villages called barrios, and roads. Civilization. We moved cautiously, expecting a Jap counterattack at every turn. That first night was black and moonless. We dug in and prepared for a Jap banzai. But none came. A couple of guys had gotten wounded, but it was probably from our own trigger-happy GIs rather than Jap snipers.

The next morning we moved out. The word was that we had to move as fast as we could. Someone said that there was a race between 1st Infantry and 1st Cavalry to see who would reach Manila first. All we knew for sure was that we had to be at a certain place by a certain time. But they didn't tell us lowly GIs where or when or why.

On the third day 2nd Battalion started to encounter Jap patrols. We set up the machine gun and took one out, maybe a half dozen soldiers. Then we broke down the gun and moved on. We learned that we were headed for the town of Villasis where the Japs had a stronghold.

"The typical barrio consisted of a single main street, a municipal building, some shops, a public gathering place, a school, an artesian well, scattered residences and sometimes a medical clinic. Residents were usually peasants who lived in town

*and farmed outside the town. Barrios were sometimes
no more than two miles apart with the space between
being open farm land, mostly rice and sugar cane.*

*"The houses were bamboo frames with palm
thatched roofs and sides, elevated about five feet off
the ground. Chickens and pigs lived under the house
and there was usually a water buffalo, or carabao, for
plowing and pulling carts. Little children rode the
carabao as they worked. Filipino day care. Carabao
had one speed...very slow. It seemed like no matter
how much you prodded them, they moved about half
the speed of a man's normal walk."*

C. B. Griggs
K Co., 1st Infantry Regt.

The whole time on the move we were getting air and
naval support. We had a naval observer with us and he called
in fire coordinates to blast any resistance we ran into. He
called back to the ships and they delivered an artillery
barrage with deadly accuracy.

Around the third day our jeeps caught up with us.
They had been pretty useless for combat in New Guinea, but
here on Luzon we actually had some roads. If they would just
stay solid enough in all the rain, they'd be a great help. Our
driver was called DB, which stood for Dry Balls. I never did
figure out why he was called that. He was an older guy,
around 40. He showed up with our jeep and trailer, and we
were all excited to get our stuff. If you had any personal
items, you put it in the trailer. Each section had its own jeep,
two jeeps for each squad, four in the platoon. But there was a
little surprise for us in our trailer. Dubbin. Here we had
thrown away all these cases of dubbin in New Guinea, and
someone else had stashed a bunch of cases in our trailer.

"DB," I said. "What are we supposed to do with all
this?"

"Hey, I'm just the driver," he said with a shrug and a smile.

We gave most of it to the Filipinos. Maybe they could figure out a use for the stuff. We quickly found out that plenty of the Filipinos were what you might call bootleggers. They made a sugar cane wine called basi. I didn't care for it, but some of the guys filled their canteens with it. I thought that was pretty stupid. There were lots of times when we didn't have enough drinking water, and here guys were lugging canteens full of sugar cane wine.

> *"There was an active passing of items back and forth between the Americans and Filipinos, sometimes offered, sometimes sold or traded. We had been issued pesos on the ship and could trade in their money. When trading or selling, the Filipinos often gave their goods to a child, appearing to be poverty stricken, to receive a better price. It seemed like all the kids had a virgin sister to sell. A lot of older Filipinos introduced themselves as guerillas from 'Maneela.'*
>
> *"At mealtime if the kitchen had caught up to us to serve a hot meal, the kids gathered around the garbage cans for scraps. At first we buried the garbage, but we got a directive to give it to the population. It was not unusual for 30 or 40 children to be at the garbage can to receive your scraps. Sometimes we'd scrape it directly into their hands to be eaten on the spot."*
>
> C. B. Griggs
> K Co., 1st Infantry

It was hot as I marched south across the rice paddies with E Company. We expected to run into heavy Jap resistance as we moved toward the Agno River, but the only problem we encountered were those pesky Jap snipers. We picked up a casualty or two from them each day, but we didn't get any organized resistance. At every town we passed

through, the residents came out to greet us. We were
liberators, throwing off three years of Japanese rule. That was
a great feeling, seeing the joy and gratitude these people had
for us. Sometimes the Filipinos asked us to help them retrieve
things they had hidden from the Japanese because they were
still around. We had orders to continue moving, but we
helped them when we could.

> *"As we crossed the Philippines we liberated
> many towns. These towns had rice stored at different
> places – in caves and throughout the countryside.
> They asked us to go with them as guards to get their
> rice."*
> Vernon Kahl
> C Co., 20th Infantry Regt.

The first real resistance we encountered was near the
town of Minien on January 12. One of our patrols was hit by
heavy artillery and automatic weapons fire from the high
ground near the town. The Japs came at us with infantry and
several light tanks from their 2nd Armor Division. But we
had caught them by surprise. We were moving so fast that we
almost overran them before either side knew what was
happening.

This was the first time we had come up against any
Jap tanks. We hammered them with machine gun fire and
knocked out two or three of them. They just stopped dead.
We couldn't figure it out. We didn't really expect the
machine guns to do much to a tank. One of the younger
guys got curious enough to sneak up to one to take a look-
see. He crawled on top of the tank and opened the hatch. He
peered into the interior for a few seconds, then jumped
down.

"They're all dead," he said. "Looks like a rivet
popped and went around in there." And that's exactly what
had happened. The light Jap tanks were riveted together. If

you hit one of the rivets with enough force, like with a machine gun bullet, it would pop and rattle around inside like a piece of shrapnel. So those light tanks turned out to be death traps.

We raced south to Villasis, taking it without much resistance. We secured our position and dug in. The Japs mounted a night banzai attack on our position, maybe about 50 or 60 of them, but we cut them down.

One of the local Filipinos came by and asked if I had cigarettes. In trade he offered up his sister, who was, of course, a virgin. I was in a joking mood. I told him I had lots of cigarettes, but it wasn't a fair trade because he only had one sister. He said that he would find another sister real quick. He wondered off and I never saw him again. Maybe he got a better deal.

A Jap suicide squad had attacked one of our SPMs (Self-Propelled Mount) just outside of Villasis and had blown one of the tracks off it. The crew had panicked after they got hit and just jumped out and abandoned it. The SPM was like an open-topped tank and Battalion wanted someone to guard it until we could bring in a tank retriever to pull it back for repairs. My platoon got the call.

We got there and the first thing I noticed was that the crew had left all their equipment, machine guns and all. The next thing I noticed was this artesian well next to what looked like some sort of school. It was spewing out beautiful fresh water and we filled our canteens. I looked at the guys. We hadn't had a bath since we left New Guinea. We looked pretty bad and smelled even worse.

"You know, you guys stink," I said. Vissher and Bradigan threw me a look that said – look who's talking. Before I left New Guinea I had taken a couple bars of laundry soap and I had one in my pack. I fished it out and cut off a chunk. It was daylight and we knew the Japs almost never attacked in daylight. So we felt safe stripping off our filthy fatigues and washing them right there. After washing them we hung everything on the tank to dry, everything but our GI boots.

So there we all were, stark naked except for our boots. All of a sudden a little Filipino kid came down the road yelling, "Japs. Japs. Many Japanese soldiers." And before we could ask him anything he took off into the bushes.

Everyone started scrambling. We had our .30-caliber water-cooled machine gun, but it was still broken down for transport and was too heavy to start dragging over and set up. The SPM had two .30-caliber light machine guns clipped to its side. I unsnapped one, threw a belt of ammunition into it, and started running down the road. Don't ask me why I did it. I don't know. I didn't think, hey, it's time to be a hero and save the platoon. I didn't think at all. Call it reflexes. Call it training. Call it anything you want. I just grabbed that gun and charged down the road.

I didn't get far before I saw the Jap patrol jogging up the road. They stopped dead when they saw me. I guess they didn't believe what they were seeing, this naked GI running toward them with a machine gun. There was a Filipino mansion nearby with a big stone wall and I figured that would be a good place to be. But so did the Japs, because they started heading for it.

I pulled the trigger on that .30-cal and just held it. It was really designed for short bursts, but I ran about two-thirds of a belt, about 200 rounds, through it, firing without stopping. The gun got red hot, but my adrenaline was flowing and I didn't even feel it. I didn't realize it at the time but my finger had gotten in the way of the bolt flying back and the impact had broken my finger. I didn't feel that either. The Japs fell down like bowling pins. Some dropped on the road, a couple crawled into the drainage ditch that ran alongside the road, and a few hightailed it into a cane field. Finally the gun got so hot I couldn't hold it any more. So I dropped it, and suddenly it dawned on me exactly how exposed my position was.

I forgot about the wall and jumped into the ditch. I landed on Jap. He was dead but his body was still quivering. I probably would have panicked from that, but I had also landed on a bunch of red ants. And in a matter of seconds they were crawling all over me. So there I was lying in the ditch and swatting like mad at those red ants. Suddenly a hand grenade rolled into the ditch right next to me. An American grenade. The rest of the squad had seen where the Japs had fled and someone had tossed a few hand grenades there. But they didn't realize I was right there among them. I reached for the grenade to toss it away, but I noticed that the pin was still in it. Whoever had thrown it was so excited he forgot to pull the pin.

Finally some of the guys came running down the road in various stages of dress. I cautiously stuck my head up. "Hey, it's me. Don't shoot." I heard shots. I stood up and saw the rest of the squad firing into the field where the Japs had fled. I ran back to the SPM, threw another belt of ammunition into the .30-caliber, and emptied it into the cane field.

We got dressed and the aid man looked at my hands. "Your hands are in pretty bad shape," he said. "The skin is all gone." He examined my finger. "And your finger is broken. You've got to go to a field hospital."

We went through the Japs to make sure they were dead and to see what we could pick up. There were 19 on the road and another 10 in the cane field. I picked up a sword from one of the officers, binoculars, a couple of pistols, flags and watches.

I went back to Battalion and to the aid station. They splinted my broken finger and put some sort of ointment on my hands before bandaging them. The doctor, a captain, said, "What the hell were you doing. Didn't you get asbestos gloves?"

I just looked at him incredulously. Obviously he thought this happened while manning a water-cooled 30. "Hell, Doc, I didn't even think about looking for gloves with the Japs coming down the road."

I stayed at the field hospital for three days. When I got out the battalion was moving out. I gave the company commander, Wheeler, one of the Jap pistols. I knew he wanted one real bad. I figured it might do me some good with him.

Right after I was released, I met with Wheeler. He asked, "How old are you, son?"

"Nineteen, sir," I said.

"Do you want to live to be 20?"

"Yes sir. I'd sure like to. I hope I live to be 25." I figured if I lived to be 25 the war would surely be over.

"Then just don't do that again."

"Someone had to do it."

"Well, there are other ways to do it."

I said, "Yes, sir." I was going to say something else but I left it at that.

"What the hell were you doing? In the first place you should be court-martialed. You were out of uniform."

"Yes sir. Everyone was."

"Why did you take off your clothes?"

"To wash them in the Artesian well."

"You were in combat. You don't do that. You should have waited for the quartermaster to come around and give you clean fatigues."

"Sometimes that never happens, sir." I said. We both knew it could be months before that happened. You turned in your old clothes to be washed and you picked up stuff that had been cleaned and that you thought would fit you. The Army just kept recycling them.

Then he told me that he was going to put me in for a medal, but he wouldn't tell me what kind. I thought I would get a Silver Star. I found out later that he put me in for a Bronze Star. And I got a Purple Heart for my hands. I was disappointed. I figured if Wheeler wasn't company commander, I would have gotten a Silver Star.

I wasn't angry because I thought my actions were any more heroic than anyone else's. I was angry because, as I thought at the time, a Silver Star got you more points toward rotation back to the States. You got one point for each month of service, five points for each beachhead, and points for medals and Purple Hearts. You also got points for children, but, of course, I didn't have any of those.

Oh well, I guess giving him that pistol didn't help after all.

> *"After the skirmish the company commander asked the guys if anyone had done anything extraordinary. We all said, 'not really.' Leonard didn't say anything either until Wheeler asked some more specific questions. I guess we all felt like we were just doing what we were supposed to do. Someone must have thought about it later and told Wheeler what Gordy had done, because we heard that he had been put in for a Bronze Star. Bronze, hell, he should have gotten a silver. As far as I'm concerned he saved all our butts that day."*
> *Mark Bradigan*
> *H Co., 1st Infantry Regt.*

Sometime after the Villasis action Lt. Johnsey called me over and said, "You're on the morning report. You are now a sergeant." That's how you got recognition in the Army; your name was mentioned in the report. Then he added, "Oh, your pay will increase, too." Other than that no one said or did anything else. There was no ceremony, just a quick comment from one of your officers. There wasn't even a change in my responsibilities. The guys in my squad were happy because they said I would have enough money now for a crap game.

Speedy Tropin started calling me sergeant. I told him, "If you do that in combat, you won't have to worry about the Japs. I'll shoot you myself. Call me Gordy." When the Japs heard sergeant or any other officer rank, you were automatically elevated to prime target. We never saluted officers on patrol or in combat for that reason.

As we moved through the barrios on Luzon we picked up bands of Filipino guerillas. Some of them were great, but some others were next to useless. They stayed with you until the shooting started and then they disappeared. We asked them for intelligence about where the Japs were and what they were doing, but we never completely trusted the information. You just never knew when they were pro Jap. The Japanese had taken good care of some of them, giving them favors and supplies.

The Filipino civilians helped us, carrying ammunition, digging slit trenches, doing odd jobs, and we gave them food or cigarettes. Most of them were solidly pro-American. But not all of them. Whenever there was a Jap counterattack, some of them would disappear, like they knew it was coming. Before the attack they'd say, "I must go find my companions. I will be back." After the attack they would return and we'd ask them if they found their companions. "No, they are gone."

Companions. Sure.

Sometimes we went through a barrio that had been shelled by our artillery. If there were wounded civilians our medics took care of them. We sent the seriously wounded to one of our field hospitals which were always within a couple of miles from where we were.

On the January 21 we received new orders. We were going to an area called the Cabaruan Hills. Another regiment of 6th Infantry, the 20th, had tried to move the Japs out of there and they had gotten hammered by well-entrenched forces. Division thought that fresh troops might be able to get the job done. The only thing we could find out from the Filipinos as we approached the area was, "Lots of Japs."

7. Back to Bataan

So E Company, with my platoon in support, headed for the Cabaruan Hills. This was a pocket of land, dominated by bamboo thickets, scrub growth and occasional palm trees, just east of where we were. The area was yet another fortified maze of caves and the Japs were dug in for a fight. A battalion of the 20th Infantry Regiment had gotten pretty well beat up trying to take the area and was finally pulled back after suffering very heavy casualties. General Edwin Patrick decided to try a two-battalion attack.

Lt. Allen, told us the bad news. He had taken over the platoon from Goldsmith who, if I recall correctly, had gotten himself killed. Allen was the opposite of Goldsmith, more like one of the guys. He was always sticking with me. He said, "You're Mr. Lucky." Not that he didn't try to get himself killed too. He was right in there with his platoon. He would joke, "Now guys, when you're digging your slit trenches, make sure you leave a little extra room just in case I have to jump in there with you."

"It's the caves," Allen said. "The Japs are dug in real deep. But somehow we've got to take it. We have requested Sherman tanks with flamethrowers, but we don't know if and when we'll get them."

The guys all looked at each other. Well, that's what we're here for.

On the way we passed barrios full of happy civilians. They offered us roast chickens which they wrapped in banana leaves. Those leaves must have acted like a preservative, because even in that heat, the chicken would last for almost a week. We gave them soap and cigarettes, and extra clothing and food if we had any. Oh yeah, we also gave them cans of dubbin. They asked if they could use it for cooking and we just said yes.

For us, Japanese resistance on the way consisted of light skirmishes and nighttime banzais. The terrain and fighting on Luzon were different than they had been in New Guinea. Here we had rice paddies and cultivated fields as well as the jungle. When we ran into an enemy patrol we had a skirmish and there was a shootout. Most of the time what was left of their patrol just disappeared into the jungle. We were constantly on the move. During the daytime there was a constant threat of snipers, and every night we were in a different hole. And there would be the inevitable banzai, maybe 50 or 60 Japs attacking our position. We usually went out in the morning to find 15 or 20 Japs dead right in front of us. But we didn't lose too many guys.

When we got into the Cabaruan Hills, we saw a tank alright, a Sherman that had come up to give us support. But the Japs had knocked it out and it was burning. The crew never got out. It was burning like a torch. It burned for a whole day.

The day after the tank had burned itself out, I happened to notice a Jap walking around it, real sneaky like. He must have been looking for something he could grab. I watched him check out the tank and then he disappeared into a cave that was nearby. Like an idiot I went in after him, not far, just enough. Luckily I surprised him. I had a .45 automatic and I aimed it right at his face. I yelled for him to surrender. He didn't have a firearm, only a sword, of which I promptly relieved him. Some officer had appropriated the first sword I had gotten at Villasis and I wanted this one.

He came out with his hands up. He was jabbering away in Japanese and I couldn't understand a word of it. I marched him down to Battalion headquarters. He must have been an officer, because some intelligence guys materialized out of nowhere and whisked him away for interrogation.

I was feeling pretty proud of myself. But that didn't last long.

The platoon sergeant, Buchong, came up and started in on me. "You ran in there, without thinking," he said. "You could have given away your position. Gotten us all killed."

I was going to let it lie; keep my mouth shut for a change. But he didn't stop. There was no love lost between the two of us.

"Give me your .45," he ordered.

"Why?"

"You're not allowed to have one anymore."

"This isn't 6th Infantry Division equipment," I countered. "I got this from the Air Corps, trading off some Japanese rifles. They had a surplus of pistols."

"Where?" he demanded.

"Back on New Guinea. Sansapor."

"What did you give them?"

"Two Japanese rifles and some other Japanese stuff."

He thought for a moment. "You can have a Tommy gun." He had a Thompson with lots of ammunition."

I wasn't in any position to argue. "OK," I said, grudgingly, and we did the swap.

Some of the guys overheard the exchange and told me that I should report Buchong when the IG came around. But I figured I was in the doghouse with him already. I didn't want to make things any worse. So I let it lie. At least I got the Thompson out of it.

Around that time the Army finally brought in a couple of tanks with flamethrowers as well as several portable flamethrowers. The Shermans had a flamethrower fitted on the front instead of a cannon and it could spew out a long, sustained stream of fire. With the portable units you only had fuel for a little more than a minute. You used it in short bursts. I picked one up, threw it on my back, and went over to where I suspected there were some Jap foxholes. I spread the flame over the area and I saw a couple of Japs run out, on fire, screaming. It wasn't very pretty, but I didn't feel bad, either. They had been just waiting for an opportunity to pick off a couple of unsuspecting GIs.

But I had gotten myself in trouble yet again. When I got back Lt. Allen pulled me aside. As I was putting down the now empty flamethrower he said, "You shouldn't have taken that. It is assigned to someone else."

Allen was a nice guy, but I must have been in a wise-guy mood. "Well there it is," I replied. "Help yourself."

It wasn't long after that little escapade that I found out that the Jap officer I captured had provided us with key information on where the main ventilation systems were for the caves in the Cabaruan Hills area. But the company commander, Wheeler, took all the credit for capturing the guy. Initially he didn't even mention me. The Army brought up some big Air Corps tanker trucks filled with napalm. Napalm is essentially gasoline mixed with something that looks like Jell-O powder. They pumped that napalm into the caves and the ventilation holes, set the stuff off, and sealed the caves. The Japs inside either burned or suffocated. We must have sealed off 2000 Japs in those caves. We attacked them with bombs, flamethrowers, bazookas, demolition charges, anything we could throw at them.

> "On one attack there was a ravine with a bamboo thicket on the other side, so thick you could hardly see anything in it. The ravine wasn't more than about a hundred yards across, and we knew the Japs were on the other side. But we couldn't see anything. A rifle platoon from F Company and a platoon of machine guns from H Company was sent in to scout around. They couldn't see anything. We put a couple of boxes of machine gun fire into the

*thicket and then we pulled back. The artillery boys
dropped a barrage into it, but all that did was blow
the tops off the bamboo. Then the Air Corps followed
up with about a dozen A20s coming in real low and
bombing the thicket.*

*"Later that day we made a push. We took the
machine guns to the northeast side. We still couldn't
see much but our orders were to put raking fire into
the field so none of the enemy could escape. We
always had two boxes of ammo ready to go, 250
rounds per belt, and the bearers were responsible for
keeping more coming.*

*"But it was a real disorganized mess. Some
of our guys were in that field too. We killed about a
thousand Japs that day, but I think that we may have
caused some friendly fire casualties too. The 1st and
20th Infantry guys coming out of that thicket were
pretty ragged. Their clothes had been all torn up from
the bamboo."*

*Mark Bradigan
H Co., 1st Infantry Regt.*

We secured the Cabaruan Hills, but it took three days
of heavy fighting and a lot of casualties to eject or kill the Japs
that were in those caves and thickets, even with the napalm.
It was much worse than New Guinea because the caves were
deeper and more heavily fortified. The cave entrances were
usually very well camouflaged and they dug their tunnels at
right angles to the opening so direct artillery fire wouldn't get
to them. You never knew when a Jap, or a whole bunch of
them, would pop out of an unseen cave or woods behind you
and start shooting or dropping mortars on you. That's what
really hurt the 20th.

*"During a mortar attack, one young guy
was afraid. "Gary, I'm scared," he said. I told him to*

stay down and he'd be OK. When I turned around
the kid was dead."
            Gary Mendoza
            A Co., 1st Infantry Regt.

Second Battalion was pulled out and we headed
south again. We crossed the Agno River, wading across the
shallow water. The crossing itself was uneventful except that
the river was full of leeches. And I mean full of them. I
knocked some off, but I just kept collecting more. There was
this one big one that scared me because it just kept getting
bigger and bigger. I tried to get it off, but he had a good hold
on me. I was careful not to break off any part of the suckers
because I didn't want it to get infected. When I reached the
river bank there was an old Filipina women with a cigar in
her mouth. She came over to me, touched the cigar to that big
old leech, and he popped right off.

As we reached the Talavera River crossing near the
town of San Jose, word spread that those Alamo Scouts along
with a detachment of Filipino guerillas, had slipped behind
enemy lines and liberated about 500 Americans held at a
prison camp near Cabanatuan. They had made their escape in
water buffalo carts, and reconnected with 6th Infantry forces
near the town of Talavera. We never saw the rangers. By the
time we got back to the staging area they had moved on to
their next assignment.

Early in the morning of February 7 there was a
massive firefight on the road between Munoz, just to the
southeast of our position, and San Jose. A Jap tank regiment
was trying to make a break out of their fortified position near
Munoz and make a run, in the predawn darkness, for the Jap
lines to the north of San Jose. But they didn't make it. We had
20th Infantry and 1st Infantry units all along that road and we
threw everything at them, .30- and .50-caliber machine guns
firing armor piercing rounds, Shermans firing 75mm shells,
company and regimental mortars, heavy 4.2 mortars, and

artillery firing 155s. We just kept blasting away. Bradigan was behind his gun. I was behind mine. Vissher was feeding belts to mine. Odell Adams was praying.

"Pray for me while you're at it," I said over the noise of the guns.

"I don't know any Jewish," he said.

"Well, just pray to God that we all make it."

When the sun came up, the entire tank regiment had been destroyed. I don't think a single vehicle made it through.

We had to make sure that the Japs in the tanks were all dead, because they sure as hell wouldn't surrender. We went up to each tank, lifted the hatch, tossed in a grenade, and closed the hatch. After that there wasn't any question.

From there our orders were to push southeast toward Manila. The word was that 1st Cavalry was having problems taking the city and we were going to join the attack. Manila. The Pearl of the Orient, they called it. That sounded pretty good.

We pushed the Japs south, and helped take Clark Field, about 40 miles northwest of central Manila. But after that, orders came that we were to divert to the west to liberate the Bataan Peninsula.

"Not Manila?" I asked. I didn't know anything about Manila except that it was a real city. Actually, I didn't know anything about Bataan either, except for the infamous Death March after the American and Filipino forces surrendered there in 1942.

"Nope. MacArthur has other plans for us. Division said that we did such a good job in the Cabaruan Hills, we're going to have the honor of liberating Bataan."

We stayed for an evening in the abandoned buildings of a World War I era cavalry base. There we found this skinny, half-starved Jap soldier. He was only a private, but whoever found him didn't shoot him, for some reason.

Battalion wanted to interrogate him anyway so we rigged up a stretcher, using two poles and some old shirts and pants, to take him down to HQ. The guys weren't happy about having to transport this Jap back. They had to carry him down a mountain trail. Every time there was a rock, they let his head bang against it. Crossing a stream, they dunked him in the water. By the time they got him to HQ, the poor guy was dead.

So we struck out to the southwest toward Bataan. Along the way we saw Red Ellis driving a supply truck. He was the guy who had shot himself in the hand at Sansapor. He stopped the truck and tossed a couple cases of supplies to us, so I guess there were no hard feelings.

Some of the supplies were rations that had all sorts of stuff, including chewing tobacco. I started passing the rations out to the guys. One of the guys in the platoon was a fellow named Bowman. He was from Arkansas and we called him Arkie. He was always wanting chewing tobacco. I took a chunk of it and I said, "Hey Arkie, how do I use this stuff?"

"You're not going to know how to use it," he said.

"Well, what do you do with it?"

"You take a big wad of it, put it in your mouth, chew it for a while, push it into your cheek and spit out the juice."

"Really, that's all there is to it?"

"Yeah," he said. "It tastes real good."

I took a chunk, put it in my mouth, chewed it for a while, pushed it into my cheek and spit out the juice. After a couple of minutes, I was so sick, I wished I had gotten shot instead. So I gave the rest of the stuff to him and another guy. They were happy to get it.

"You want some cigarettes, instead?" Arkie asked.

"Uh, no. I don't think I want anything to do with tobacco."

Every little barrio we went through, the Filipinos came out to greet us with waving hands and wide smiles. The villagers spoke various dialects of the indigenous language, Tagalog, and most of them spoke some English and some Spanish. In one barrio this old guy came up to me. "Hey, Joe, you got cigaretto?"

I handed him a pack of cigarettes. I didn't smoke and I was happy to give them to the villagers.

"Thanks, Joe. You got soap?" I had some laundry soap in my pack and I handed him a bar. I think they really wanted soap for washing themselves, but the stuff I gave him was laundry soap that had lye in it. "What do you want for it," he asked. "You want pom pom?" That was their term for a girl.

"No I don't want pom pom. Too dangerous."

"What do you want?"

"You got chicken?"

He smiled. "Roasted?"

"Yeah, cooked," I said.

"I got," he said. "I got eggs too." And he gave me a roasted chicken and a half dozen eggs.

I gave the eggs to the kids that were hanging around and I took the chicken back to share with the squad. "Hey, how'd you get this?" they wanted to know. I told them about the cigarettes and the soap.

Some of the guys were disappointed. As always, they were looking for alcohol. There was some Manila whiskey around; a bottle or two of that would show up occasionally as well as Filipino beer. And there was basi, the homemade sugar cane wine. It was pretty rough. Then we discovered that there was another wine-like liquor made from coconuts. It was supposed to be better then basi. I couldn't tell you because I stayed away from all of it.

A lot of the Jap motor pools had run out of gasoline and they were running some of their vehicles on alcohol. Some industrious Filipinos were draining the Jap gas tanks, filling liquor bottles, and selling it to the GIs. No one in my squad went for it, but I heard that a couple of GIs went blind after drinking the stuff. I warned my guys no to touch it.

Second Battalion moved onto the Bataan Peninsula at Orani against scattered resistance. We were getting artillery rounds dropped on us occasionally and we couldn't tell where they were coming from. As we moved in, we passed a lot of big churches and someone noticed that the doors on some of the churches were covered with smoke stains. We finally figured out where the Japs were hiding their artillery. Some of these little towns we passed through, it turned out, were pro Jap, and the good citizens had forgotten to mention that the Japs were hiding their artillery pieces in the churches. So we started breaking into the churches, and if we found any Japs or artillery, we torched the whole thing. It weighed on the conscience of some of the more religious guys for a while...but not for long.

We had orders to be in the town of Orion by February 11 in coordination with an amphibious assault on the southern tip of the peninsula around Mariveles, scheduled for February 12. But as we moved to the east coast of the peninsula at Pilar, we learned that the amphibious forces wouldn't be ready in time. The assault was postponed to February 15. From Pilar, we moved south along the coast to Orion. We dug in, alongside E Company, on the south side of the town. My machine guns were set up on one side of a bridge that crossed a canal. On our right was the defensive perimeter for Battalion headquarters. We had been getting air drops of equipment and supplies, and just inside the battalion perimeter we had stockpiled 55-gallon drums of gasoline and cases of mortar shells.

On the night of the 15th the Japs attacked our position, just as it was getting dark. It seemed like they were coming from every direction. A bunch of what first looked like civilians came down the road, and some came out of the Filipino cemetery. It turns out that the Japs had built tunnels under this old cemetery. The "civilians" were Japs and they were trying to penetrate the headquarters perimeter. Then we saw little boats coming up the canal, carrying some Japanese soldiers. They must have come from one of the wrecked ships still sitting out in Manila Bay.

All hell broke loose. We were firing at anything that looked like a Jap. Men were running and falling everywhere. The Japs broke through the perimeter and blew up the gasoline dump. The fires made eerie shadows and silhouettes, and it was hard to tell who was who. One of our guys, Risty Kostov, tried to jump over a wall. The fire was behind him and he was all lit up. Jap machine gun fire practically cut him in two. Poor guy. He was from Yugoslavia and had been drafted. I don't think he was even a U.S. citizen. A guy from another squad, Offermann, was firing away at the attackers, but he went down in a hail of Jap bullets.

Some of the burning gasoline found its way into the canal and into the bay, setting some barges on fire. The flames under the bridge where we were made it terribly hot. We continued slapping belts into the machine gun and firing, but everyone seemed to be running in every direction. There was so much confusion. I didn't want to take the chance of hitting any of our guys, so I decided to dump the machine gun and take off. I finished the belt, then pulled the back plate off the gun. We dumped it in the river and my crew and I took off down a little trail. We figured we'd get up the trail a bit, then regroup. When we looked back, Battalion headquarters was lit up like a giant homecoming bonfire. Exploding mortar shells were going off in every direction. It was just chaos.

My crew took off in all directions. I found a place behind a church and sat behind the wall trying to figure out what to do. I figured I would wait until daylight and then see what I could do. I didn't want to go up into the hills because you didn't know what, or who, was up there. Two other GIs, from another company, found their way to the church wall with me, and we awaited the dawn together. When daylight came things started to get organized. There were bodies all over the place, some burned beyond recognition.

After it was all over, we realized that the local Filipinos had all left town before the attack. They said they were going up into the hills to retrieve their belongings that they had hidden from the Japanese. We thought that's what they were doing. But they had known there was going to be a counterattack and they had pulled out. I think they came back expecting to see the Japanese instead of Americans.

We had some Filipino guerillas with us. Their leader was a self-appointed colonel and he decided these villagers were pro Jap. And there was only one thing to do with pro Japs. He gave the order to execute them. The guerillas took a bunch of them, maybe 50, down to a church. They just shot them all. When MacArthur learned about the executions he was furious. He said, "You let them kill innocent people." And we had no answer. He wanted the Filipino guerillas rounded up and shot, but we didn't want to do it, and we didn't have any way to do it even if we wanted to. The American colonel, I think his name was Smith, was relieved of command and sent back to New Guinea for allowing it to happen. Supposedly it was his responsibility as a ranking Army officer to stop any civilian executions. But who knows? It was war time. Your values get distorted. No one knew what was going on. MacArthur was so angry he ordered continuous combat for the entire 1st Infantry Regiment.

The GIs in 1st Infantry started calling the Filipinos Mac's Little Brown Brothers and Sisters. It probably wasn't fair – most of the Filipinos were decidedly pro American – but we had lost good men on Bataan and we were sore.

It was on Bataan that I saw the great man himself for the first and only time. We had had a banzai attack the night before and I was manning the machine gun the next day. Word came down that a high-ranking officer was coming through and we were alerted to be on our best behavior. MacArthur came by our position flanked by four other officers. He was all dressed up in real fancy clothes and he had his trademark corncob pipe. His hat was all beat up.

"How many Japs did you kill?" he asked me.

"I know we killed some sir," I replied. "But I don't know how many. We didn't go out and count them."

"Hm. What's your position?"

"Section sergeant, heavy machine guns."

"Where's the other section sergeant?"

"He got wounded up in the hills, so I'm taking care of both sections right now."

'Did you get promoted for it?" he asked. "Talk to the company commander to give you the right promotion."

I was going to tell him that Wheeler wouldn't do it, but I didn't want to cause any trouble. "That's OK. Just leave everything the way it is."

And then he was off talking to some of the other guys. He wanted to know if we knew of any Filipinos killing their own people. Nobody said a word. We knew they were doing it, but we didn't want to say anything. Then he got back in his jeep and drove off. Well, at least I had gotten to see the great MacArthur. Some of the officers didn't think much of him. He was really tough on everybody. He would break an officer for no good reason at all if he didn't get what he wanted. But he was the man in command.

Since we suspected that some of the attacking Japs were coming from a big hulk lying offshore, and might be using it as they retreated, the Navy sent in a PT boat to sink it with torpedoes. One of the torpedoes found its mark. But the other missed and headed for shore where some of us GIs were stationed along a sea wall. Instead of abandoning the wall, we fired on the torpedo with rifles and machine guns as it sped toward us. Of course we couldn't hit it and we finally scattered like rabbits as the torpedo neared the sea wall. Luckily, it hit the seawall at an angle, bounced off it, ran for a while, then suddenly stopped dead. It had gotten hung up in shallow water. If that torpedo had hit the seawall head-on enough to detonate, I might not be alive to tell the story.

From Orion we moved west, cutting across the Bataan Peninsula. In the beginning we didn't know too much about what happened there other than what we had seen in the indoctrination films. Some of the guys were scared because MacArthur couldn't hold Bataan in 1942 with three or four divisions. And here we were, one regiment, half shot up, assigned to take it back from the Japs.

> *"We used some of the same roads that the prisoners used on the Bataan Death March going in the opposite direction. We passed some of the wells from which they couldn't drink. We saw some of the same Filipino people. In 1942 civilians were shot for offering food or water to the prisoners. This time they waved American flags and flashed the V for Victory sign. Children asked us if we had 'any gum chum?'"*
> C. B. Griggs
> K Co., 1st Infantry Regt.

As we passed through the barrios, the villagers told us how the Japanese had mistreated our guys. If they fell down on the march, most of them were bayoneted or beheaded. The villagers also told us how cruel the Japanese soldiers were to the villagers, raping the women and killing those they found, or even suspected of, helping the prisoners in any way.

We asked them if there were any Japs around now.

"Oh yes. Over there." They would point in a general direction.

"Where?"

"Over there." They wouldn't get any more specific than that. They wouldn't say exactly where they were. Maybe they didn't know. Maybe there were hedging their bets in case the Japs came back.

So we would send out a patrol with machine guns as backup. We'd find them, eliminate them, and move on. Their dead were left where they lay. Our dead were carried back and watched until GRO could pick them up. And of course they counterattacked at night.

> *"One night I had to go out on patrol... We went out, went along, soon we heard a noise in the ditch. We three guys hit the ground. I heard three safeties go off. We listened. The noisemaker moved a little bit. We couldn't figure out what was going on. My heart was pounding so hard that I thought the enemy could hear it. I was that scared. Soon a wild hog came out of the ditch! That's what had made the noise. It sure scared the heck out of us."*
> *Vernon Kahl*
> *C Co., 20th Infantry Regt.*

After we killed the enemy, we went through their stuff for anything of intelligence, and souvenirs of course. Then, since the bodies started deteriorating so fast, we got away from them as quickly as we could. If one was lying there wounded you would have to kill him, because we couldn't treat them, and we certainly couldn't trust them.

Early on one of our officers – who wasn't in the front-line combat by the way – said, "We're not going to waste bullets on them. Just stick them with the bayonet on your rifle."

"But sir, "I countered. "I'm a machine gunner. I don't have a rifle."

"Then get one. One you hit a live one he'll scream out and then you can kill him."

"You know," I replied, "With all the bullets we fire through the machine gun during an attack, we can always afford a bullet for each Jap to make sure he is dead."

He seemed satisfied with that.

So we started shooting the bodies, especially after a major banzai attack, raking them with machine gun fire to make sure that they were all dead. But what was there to do with all the bodies that piled up, sometimes on a nightly basis? We just left them there. After a major banzai, if we were pinned down for a while, the odor would get terrible. But we couldn't do anything about it. We tried to push them as far away from us as we could. Eventually we would bring up an armored bulldozer – it had to be armored in case the Japs were still around – dig a ditch, push the bodies in, and push the dirt back over them. That was it.

One time near a barrio a bunch of Filipinos were trying to kill a carabao. They were hitting it on the head with a maul and not doing much good. Bradigan went up to them and told them to try hitting it between the eyes. They gave it one whack and the carabao went down. Then they slit its throat to kill it. They were thankful and wanted to give us some carabao milk, but we said no thanks. We weren't going to drink anything that wasn't pasteurized.

Another time, we were guarding bridges and the battalion set up near this little town. A couple of guys went in to town and there was a wedding in progress. Some ladies came by and asked if we could fire our guns. They said it was a sign of good luck to fire a gun. The sergeant, Bill Cordeville, from Kansas City, Missouri, said, "Bradigan why don't you fire a clip up into the coconut tree." So Bradigan emptied a clip. But we were so close to the Battalion CP that they heard the shots. They got all riled up until they found out what had happened. Major Meyers, Battalion commander, told Wheeler, "Tell the guys not to take part in any more wedding ceremonies." So the word went out, but most of the guys had no idea what they were talking about.

It didn't take us long to secure the peninsula. After all our fears about Bataan, we encountered only scattered resistance as we moved west. I guess Bataan was a lot more important to us than it was to the Japanese. We reached the coast at Bagac on February 21. But no sooner had we arrived there, we received orders to move out. All we knew for sure was that we were headed for the mountains north of Manila. Rumor had it, however, that General Yamashita had evacuated from Manila into his mountain defensive stronghold and we were going to attack him.

Elsewhere in the Pacific Theater

In February, after three months of preparatory bombing, the U.S. Marines invaded Iwo Jima, beginning a bloody five-week battle to take the island. Air Corps long-range B29s began the firebombing of Tokyo, destroying 50% of the city by war's end. In March the Army invaded the island of Midanao, continuing the reconquest of the Philippines.

8. Chasing Yamashita

By the beginning of March we had moved into the watershed area northeast of Manila, and had entered the town of Montalban. Wheeler, H Company commander, had been replaced, for some reason, buy a guy named Mollinger. I certainly wasn't sorry to see him go. Mollinger was promoted from a rear echelon position. He was an older guy, a gung-ho captain. He believed in being right up front all the time to find out what was going on. He said, "We're going to fight as a team. I understand that Wheeler didn't have many friends. Maybe that's the way he thought it had to be. But we will all work together." During one particularly heavy Jap counterattack he was wounded in the groin. When the medics took him away he was moaning that he would never be able to have children. Mollinger was replaced by Curtis Johnsey. Johnsey was the opposite of Wheeler. He was fair and really cared for the guys in the company. They never promoted Johnsey from 1st lieutenant to captain. He just took over the company.

There wasn't much resistance in Montalban, and taking the town was pretty uneventful. It was the area beyond the town that scared us. The land beyond Montalban rose in a group of mountains. They weren't very high – the highest ones were maybe 1000 feet – but they were very steep, heavily wooded, and heavily fortified. In addition to their normal assortment of lethal fortifications the Japanese had installed some big naval guns in those hills and they had been using them to devastating effect. Rumor had it – of course we always seemed to get more rumors than facts –

that Yamashita had taken the guns when he captured Singapore. Well, no matter where they came from, we had to push the Japs off those mountains and those guns had to go.

My platoon was held in the town as part of a reserve force to support attacks into the hills by elements of the 63rd and 20th Infantry Regiments. There weren't any organized counterattacks against Montalban, but the Japs were shelling the town, sometimes from those big guns. And for the first time we were shelled by rockets. They had a 17-inch rocket that they fired from a V-type wooden platform. I think the Germans gave them the rockets.

The Japs rolled those big naval guns out of their hiding places in the daytime, fired them, then pulled them back in. So you couldn't see where the damn things were. We tried sending spotter planes up into the hills, but the Japs pulled the guns back in too fast. We lost a couple of planes in the process. We sent air strikes into the hills, but they weren't having any affect, not on the guns anyway. Division sent a couple of companies up into the hills, but for the meantime, we stayed in reserve in Montalban.

While we were in Montalban someone came across a Jap motorcycle sitting among their abandoned equipment. A little searching turned up about a hundred of these little Jap motorcycles, some with sidecars. We gassed those things up and were playing around on them like a bunch of kids, riding them up and down the streets. It was like – who knew there was a war on? We were having a hell of a time. Every once in a while a couple of rockets came down and everyone in the vicinity jumped off the motorcycles, often falling into a ditch or rice paddy. Then we all got up and jumped on the nearest motorcycle, or went back and got another one. We did have a guy get hurt because we didn't know how to operate the sidecars. All the labels were in Japanese. He was zipping along in the passenger car and he yanked the lever that detached the car. The car went flying, with a startled GI hanging on for dear life. He was shaken up, but he was lucky he didn't get killed. We packed him off to the aid station and then resumed our frivolity. Boy it sure felt good to let loose, pretend that you were somewhat normal, at least for a little while.

The Japs were really entrenched in those hills beyond the town and the men we had sent up there were taking a heavy beating. They attacked up the slopes and they did spot the guns. But they couldn't make it to the top. The Japs were just too tough. They counterattacked furiously and we started running low on supplies...and men.

> "This was very hilly terrain and presented us with a different kind of warfare. The procedure was to move up a hill, and if we drew enemy fire on the way up, have the hill bombed and shelled. Then try again. If we made it, repeat the process with the next hill. Meanwhile, dig in and wait for a road to be built to bring up supplies. We could expect sniper fire and mortar and artillery fire from the next hill each day. While we waited for the road, we mostly stayed in our holes, not making easy targets for enemy snipers.
>
> "Before moving to the next hill we had two days' supply of food. The big problem was water. At the foot of each hill there was usually a stream. To get water, six or seven men carrying 10 or 12 canteens and escorted by two or three armed guards went to the bottom of the hill for water. We called these Jack and Jill trips, except they went down the hill to fetch water."
>
> C. B. Griggs
> K Co., 1st Infantry Regt.
>
> "[At night] I slept in a three-man hole, a good-sized hole – big enough for Doc Ziglar, Rhodes, and myself. Our company mortar section used that

hole the next morning from which to fire their
mortars. That day an enemy shell landed in the hole
and killed three of the boys there – the foxhole I'd
slept in the night before."
          Vernon Kahl
          C Co., 20th Infantry Regt.

So the rest of us were ordered in. We started up the
slopes of one of those damn mountains. Sixth Division was
attacking up Mt. Mataba and Mt. Pacawagan. The platoon
sergeant just pointed and said, "We're going up there," and
that's where we went. To me they both looked about the
same…harbingers of death…but from the looks of things, I
thought we were heading up Mt. Mataba.

> *Leonard and the rest of the foot soldiers of*
> *the 6th Division didn't know it but they were*
> *attacking the defenses of the Japanese Shimbu Group.*
> *General Yamashita had divided his forces on Luzon*
> *into three groups in three geographical regions. The*
> *forces designated as the Shobu group consisted of*
> *around 150,000 troops in northern Luzon,*
> *commanded by Yamashita himself. The Kembu*
> *Group had around 30,000 troops in the area around*
> *Clark Field. And the Shimbu Group had around*
> *80,000 troops in a large area including the*
> *mountains outside Manila. In late February, General*
> *Walter Krueger, commander of the U.S. Sixth Army,*
> *directed the 6th and 43rd Infantry Divisions, the 1st*
> *Cavalry Division, and the 112th Cavalry Regimental*
> *Combat Team to drive the Japanese of the Shimbu*
> *Group out of their mountain strongholds.*

We fought the Japs in those mountains for two bloody
months. We'd get up there and they would beat us back
down. We'd move off to the side slopes and they'd pour

shells on us from the peaks. The whole time, we were attacking up, and they were shooting down at us.

Around this time we got word that we were going to get some entertainment. We figured maybe we'd finally get some movie stars. They were always promising movie stars but we never got any. But this time they said a reinforced convoy was coming through and we were going to get movie stars. No girls, though, much to our disappointment. They said it was still too dangerous to bring the girls in. A couple of days later Joe E. Brown came through with his band and put on a great show for us. He was really friendly with all of the troops. Someone said that his son had been killed fighting in Europe. But he put on a great show for us and spent time with us, thanking us, telling us to keep on fighting. He posed for pictures and I have one of him sitting on my knee. Later I learned that his son, who was in the air corps had, in fact, been killed, but that he had died in 1942.

On one attack up the hill to reach some stranded troops, we got about halfway up. But the Jap mortar and automatic weapon fire was just too much. E Company was up there and we were trying to give them support. We were moving up a steep, wooded slope. I was carrying the water-cooled machine gun receiver with a bipod, and I had my own carbine and a .45. The ammo bearers were carrying the chests of ammunition. The Japs opened up with a heavy barrage of 150mm mortars.

A mortar exploded right next to me. I lost my balance and dropped the machine gun. Sliding down the hill, I grabbed for anything that might stop my fall, to no avail. After sliding about two or three hundred feet I managed to grab onto a bush. That stopped my fall, but the machine gun came tumbling down and hit me in the chest. If that wasn't enough, a chest of ammunition followed it, hitting me in the back.

Doc Mullins came sliding down to me. Let me tell you. These medics were a fantastic bunch. Even under heavy fire, they would try to get to you and they'd administer aid while the bullets were flying by. "We've got to get up. We've got to get up," he said.

"My leg," I said. I had suddenly become aware of a searing pain in my leg.

I hadn't realized it at first but I had taken a piece of shrapnel in my leg. Mulllins quickly cut my fatigues, pulled out the shrapnel and tossed it away. Luckily it wasn't in very deep.

"Hey, maybe I wanted that as a souvenir," I said, half jokingly. He just gave me one of those you-can't-be-serious looks, slapped at big bandage on it, and pulled me up. "By the way, I think you have broken ribs," he added. "But I can't do anything for that."

We broke off the attack. On the way down, we took everything we could carry. I didn't know what condition that big .30-cal. was in after tumbling down the hillside, so I chucked it into a ravine. There were dead GIs scattered on the hillside and if you wanted to grab a rifle, you took it. My ribs hurt like hell, but I strapped my carbine across my back and picked up a case of grenades. I figured if we got pinned down, there was nothing like a nice load of hand grenades. They were the best.

The Army tried to supply the stranded troops with air drops, but the Japs wound up getting most of the supplies. We lost radio communication with them. Later, we found out that that the Japs had finally surrounded them and wiped them out.

It was during this time that we lost our division commander, General Edwin Patrick, and our regimental commander, Colonel James Rees. We were continuing to attack eastward, the Japs still in possession of the mountain tops. The Japs were throwing furious night banzais at us. If there wasn't a moon at night, we knew we would be getting a banzai attack. Usually it was pitch dark and the artillery guys sent up paraflares, flares slung on parachutes that would light up the whole area with an eerie light. You could see them crawling around out there, but they could also see you.

We were in our foxholes but we wanted some extra protection. So we got an airdrop including food, supplies, sandbags and barbed wire. We set up the barbed wire and it did help against the counterattacks. We also set out some of our homemade hand grenade mines in front of us. Of course the problem in the morning was finding the hand grenades that we had set out, and disarming them without blowing ourselves up.

One morning, after a major banzai, General Patrick showed up with his entourage. I couldn't believe it. This was a frontline area and here comes Patrick all dressed up in his bright, new Khaki outfit that he always wore. We were dressed in drab khakis, not the greatest fashion statement, but certainly better for keeping a low profile in combat. We had just had a major banzai attack and snipers were all over the place. Just beyond our position the dead Japs were stacked pretty high. Of course we knew that a field of dead Japs wasn't necessarily a field of ALL dead Japs.

Patrick was down the line a bit, so I didn't see exactly what happened. One guy who was there said that Patrick saw a Jap officer out among the dead and he was interested in any papers the officer might have on him. Another guy said it was the Jap's sword he was after. In any event, the machine gunners sprayed the bodies around the officer. Then the mortar guys dropped a couple of shells in for good measure.

But apparently they didn't spray the trees. That's where the sniper was. A burst of machine gun fire took out both Patrick and Rees before the sniper was cut down. I didn't know anything about Patrick, nor much about Rees for that matter. They may have been tactical military geniuses, for all I knew, but they sure didn't show much smarts coming out to the forward area like that. This was the front line, and he was out there like a newly-arrived soldier. Why didn't he just put a great big target on his back? And seeing that Jap officer should have raised a red flag. The Japs tried to carry their officers back with them. That one in the pile was a good candidate for a booby trap or a magnet for a sniper.

General Charles Hurdis took over for Patrick and Colonel Corbin, from 1st Battalion, took over the regiment. But for us guys on the ground, it was business as usual.

We kept attacking up the slopes. Getting supplies sometimes became problematic. One time up in those hills we went three days without fresh water. That was horrible. I had gone up with two full canteens and I was down to my last couple of swallows. They finally reached us with big Lister bags full of wonderful fresh water. Most of us, including me, filled our canteen cups and quaffed down the water, although we knew we weren't supposed to do it. The shock of that sudden intake of water made us cramp up. We couldn't talk. They told us to take sips, don't drink or it will knock you out. It was true.

> *"My luck finally ran out. On March 9 a mortar shell landed behind me and I took a piece of shrapnel in my posterior thigh. I think the doc made a bigger wound cutting it out than the original shrapnel. I told Whitlock, a friend from West Monroe, Louisiana, to hold my mail while I was in the hospital. I was out of action for two months. When I returned, I learned that Whitlock had been killed a week after I was hit."*
> C. B. Griggs
> K Co., 1st Infantry

Still moving around to the east, we came to a downward-sloping terraced area that would soon be dubbed Devil's Stepladder. We fought down into the different levels, surrounded by the Japanese, for two weeks straight. Shenkel got a piece of shrapnel in his face. The medics took him back down and we didn't see him for a while. The banzais came almost every night. Then every day, we tried to ferret them out of their hiding places and fortifications. One day we sent out a patrol and it didn't come back. We sent out a platoon to look for them and my machine gun squad went with them.

We found the unfortunate patrol. It looked like some of them had been killed by mortar fire. The rest had been bayoneted with their hands tied behind their backs. Some of them looked like their heads had been almost chopped off. They were just kids, my age. I recognized one of the guys. I had met him on the ship going over to New Guinea. But I didn't even know his name. He had been blown in two by a mortar shell. His binoculars were still around the top half of his body.

For some reason we had a Catholic chaplain with us on the patrol. I think the Army sent him along with us because they knew there were some dead GIs out there. He calmly said, "Please gather the bodies, boys, I'm going to give them last rites."

One of the guys asked, "What if they're Jewish, Father?"

"I know how to speak Hebrew and I can recite the Kaddish," he replied. The Kaddish is the Jewish prayer for the dead.

"You do?" I asked him.

"Yes, I do," he replied.

"I don't know it and I'm Jewish," I said in amazement.

"Let's get all these bodies gathered up as quickly as we can," said the chaplain. "We're going to try to get a truck down here. We're going to load these bodies on the truck and get them out of here." Luckily there was a road nearby that a small truck could navigate.

"Let's go, boys. They're dead, and they're feeling no pain, so don't be scared." He pulled a pair of heavy mortician's gloves from his pack. "They are not feeling anything now. They are with God. You can't hurt them. Be sure you get them in the bags and get a tag off each one."

We didn't have any body bags, but the guys had their mattress covers that we got when we went overseas. We picked up the bodies, took off the name tags, and placed them in the mattress covers. They had already been dead a couple of days and they had started to decompose. A couple of the guys in our patrol just couldn't do it. They were crying. No one said an unkind word to them.

The chaplain said a prayer over each body. He looked at the dog tag to see what religion they were and then said the appropriate prayer. One of the guys turned out to be Jewish and he did say the Kaddish for him.

We attacked again, trudging up the mountain. We had a company on top and we were trying to give them support. On the way up we set up the machine gun. The Japs hit us with a mortar barrage and automatic weapon fire. They also had some of those 17-inch rockets that the Germans had given them. But they didn't have proper launchers. They just laid them down and fired them and they went wild, all over the place.

During the attack, in the confusion I didn't realize that the rest of the squad had withdrawn down the hill. And they didn't realize I was still up there. I was the only one with the gun at the time. I thought the other guys were right behind me.

Normally you needed two guys to operate the machine gun, one to feed the belt and the other to fire the gun. But one man can do it easily if you have to. I just fed the belts into the gun, one right after the other. I must have fired

14 or 15 belts. The entire time I thought the rest of the squad was right behind me, but in reality they were 100 or so yards down the ridge. I had no idea they were that far away and that I was so far ahead of them. There was heavy brush all over, especially ahead where the Japs were, and I just kept traversing the area.

I fired away with the machine gun at the Jap positions until a Jap mortar scored a direct hit on the gun. I was blown out of the machine gun emplacement and the gun was destroyed. I was knocked out for a moment. When I regained consciousness, my helmet was crushed and I had a cut from the shrapnel in my forehead, right above my eye. It left a big bump on my forehead that I can still feel today.

I should have thanked my lucky stars that I wasn't killed, but my first thought was what a waste it was that we had carried that damned machine gun all the way up that hill and now it was wrecked. The guys clambered back up to me and helped me down to the aid station. They cleaned up my eye with alcohol. Boy did that burn. And that was it.

I didn't know it at the time but somebody told the company commander what had happened and I would get another Bronze Star commendation for that action. That would make three. I got one for defending the SPM at Villasis, one for capturing the Japanese officer in the Cabaruan Hills – I finally got credit for that – and one for the solo machine gun stunt in the hills near Montalban. But I didn't think of myself as any kind of hero. I was just one guy doing what he had to do.

> *"He [Wyatea] shot only once, killing someone; but then his gun jammed. We think he shot the guy who threw at us what must have been a bundle of dynamite! Wyatea was a Native American who didn't talk real plain. I heard him say, 'Sgt. Tall. Sgt. Tall. Bring your rifle! Mine don't work!' He was a guy who didn't take the best care of his equipment.*

*I brought my rifle down to him. It wasn't long after
that the assistant BAR team used up most of their
ammunition. They knew that Sgt. Kahl always
carried two bandoliers of ammunition, besides what's
on the belt. They wanted more ammunition. I crawled
over to them and give[sic] them my extra
bandoliers."*
        Vernon Kahl
        C Co., 20th Infantry Regt.

*"I'll make no bones about it, I was scared
most of the time, but I never ran. I saw old combat
guys break and run. Normally, once I started
shooting, the fear left me. I was NOT a hero! Just a
'grunt.' I did earn the Combat Infantry Badge, and
the Bronze Star. I foolishly refused the Purple Heart."*
        Milton Galke
        E Co., 1st Infantry Regt.

We kept pushing forward by day. The Japs kept
counterattacking at night. With almost every counterattack in
that engagement we were in real danger of being overrun.
Some of the guys got scared and stopped firing their guns. If
the Japs did break through your position we just lay flat in
our slit trench and waited until morning, hoping they
wouldn't come by. Then when you popped your head up to
look around, if anything didn't look right, you shot it. I had to
do that a couple of times. One time was at Devil's Stepladder.

Ordinance had come by that day to check our guns
and they gave us new barrels. You couldn't see it too well in
the daytime, but at night you could follow the tracers. If they
were falling short, you knew that your barrel was burned out.
After you had put two or three thousand rounds through one
of those barrels, they were pretty well burned out, even with
the water-cooling jacket. The barrels got so hot that we used
asbestos gloves to handle them. Of course asbestos is
poisonous in the long term, but nobody knew about it at the

time. Changing the barrel at night was a real chore so we tried to do it in the daytime whenever possible.

We got new barrels for two of the guns. We took them apart and replaced the barrels. I was sitting behind one of the guns. It worked perfectly. But I only fired a couple of rounds through it. I should have fired some more, but I figured it was OK.

That night I sat behind the gun, waiting for the Japs to come. Mark Bradigan was up there with me along with Odell Adams and Harold Vissher. The machine gun was in the center and we had our two side holes dug off at an angle. Adams was supposed to be first gunner, but he was a very religious guy and he was praying that night. I said, "Just pray this damn gun works."

When the Japs came, and they got close enough, I pulled the trigger. The gun fired two rounds...and jammed. We cleared the jam and put the belt back in. I fired two rounds, and it jammed again. Buchong said, "We're going to get overrun tonight," and he disappeared into the night. No matter what we did to that gun, we couldn't get it to fire more than one or two rounds before it jammed. We even tried different belts, thinking maybe there was something wrong with a couple of them. Nothing worked. This was one of the worst banzais we had, and my damn gun wouldn't fire.

We had a load of grenades with us so we started tossing them out there. Some of them were rifle grenades, but we didn't have any of the cartridges needed to fire them. So every couple of minutes we tossed a grenade out into the darkness. We did that all night. I also had my Garand and I fired it out toward any sound I heard. I don't know if I ever hit anything with it, though. The Japs had gotten behind us, but they were wiped out by the riflemen.

Shenkel was at gun number two. His gun was firing perfectly, although he did get wounded some time that night.

We found out later that he hadn't changed his barrel. Shenkel figured it was firing short already and he would just compensate for that.

The next morning we checked out the gun. I was going to complain to ordinance. But it fired perfectly, like a brand new gun. There were about 25 or 30 dead Japs in front of our position, and I thought I'd go out and check for souvenirs.

Buchong saw me. He said, "Where are you going?"

"I'm going to check the Japs."

"Like hell you are. I'll shoot you if you go out there."

"Why?" I asked.

"Let the riflemen go out there," he said.

"I want to see what we did. After all it was a very dangerous night."

But he was firm. "You're not going out there."

So a squad of riflemen went out to check the bodies. When they came back one had a sword, and the others had an assortment of souvenirs.

"Hey, that's my stuff. I killed them."

"No it ain't. We took it off the dead ones."

"They're all dead?"

"Yep, they're all dead. You did a good job."

It must have all been from the grenades, because I don't think I hit anything with my Garand.

When we were in combat the kitchens tried to get chow up to us. One morning, after they had brought up breakfast, one of the guys called me over. "Hey Gordy, we've got a guy for your platoon." It was a replacement and he was from the south side of Chicago.

And he was pissed. Apparently he had been in the quartermaster corps and they had pulled him out as a replacement. "How the hell did I get into this," he said angrily. "I want to get transferred. I want to go back to what I was doing."

"Hey," I said. "I had nothing to do with that. If you want to complain about it, you'll have to go see the company commander."

He was thinking about it.

"Look," I said. "We just got breakfast, and the Japs are pretty smart. They know about what time we get our food. So the food is down at the bottom of the ridge. Go get your mess kit and get some."

"I came from the quartermaster corps," he said. "I'm not going to eat these powdered eggs and dehydrated spuds. I've got some of my own stuff I brought."

"I wouldn't go broadcasting that. If everyone knew they'll be asking you to share it." Since he wasn't budging, I gave him some advice. "OK, start digging your hole right next to mine. Make sure it's deep enough. And pray that we don't get hit by mortar or artillery fire. The Japs have been hitting us just about every day."

I left him and went down the ridge. I figured I'd get a big mess kit full of whatever we had and give him some of it. While I was gone the Japs opened up with 150mm mortars. One landed right where the kid was. They never found enough of him to bury. I don't even know who he was.

I felt sorry for the kid, but what really made me angry was that my pack was lying next to him in the hole and I had a Jap flag with sunrays coming out of the circle. They were really hard to come by. And it had gotten blown to pieces. "The bastards," I yelled. "Look what they did." I guess that's a sad commentary on how callous we had become to people dying around us.

Another time I got mad at the Japs was over a poncho, of all things. We had just gotten new ponchos issued to us, really good ones. The rainy season was coming in and I was glad to have a new poncho. But it was a little mildewed, so I laid it out flat to dry in the sun. The Japs opened up on us with mortars and it took a direct hit. I shook my fist and yelled up into the hills, "You bastards. I'm not going to forgive you for this. I needed a new poncho and now I don't have one."

"I arrived on Luzon as a replacement in April 1945. We went to a staging area just before the Sierra Madre Mountains. We were near an artillery battery, howitzers. That evening, the sergeants came and called names and put guys in different groups. About 20 of us were assigned to Co C. The sergeants took us to trucks and issued us all M1 rifles, helmets and bandoliers of ammunition. They said, 'Don't do anything with this until we tell you what to do.' We went to a makeshift target range, lit up with truck lights because it was getting dark. The sergeants said, 'Lock and load. Zero in your weapons.'

"We slept on the warm ground that evening. Then next morning we saw guys moving up into the hills. The sergeant said, 'That's where we're going.' We loaded up on trucks and went into the hills. About two thirds up the mountain we saw our first dead bodies. They were Japanese, rotting in the heat. I got a little sick. The platoon sergeants were very supportive. I was assigned to carry ammo for a BAR man, Lesk, from Wheeling West Virginia. Then we started seeing American bodies. They were under ponchos with tags.

"We got to the top of the ridge. As soon as we got to the top everyone was shooting, so I started shooting too. But I wasn't sure what I was shooting at. We set up the machine guns and set about our assignment to keep the highway below, if you could call it that, clear of Japanese. All of a sudden we came under mortar fire and I was wounded by a mortar shell. The flat part of a fragment cut my lip. The aid man treated me and I wasn't out of action more than a couple of hours.

"The first American I saw get killed was a scout. We were going up through a ravine – a five man scout team. When we got to the top I went left and Voltz went right. A Jap in a stand-up foxhole with a cover shot Voltz in the butt. We killed the Jap and set up a perimeter around Voltz. He was joking that he had a stateside wound. But he was bleeding internally and he died in front of us. Sergeant Rogers simply said, 'He's gone.' Voltz was always kidding around. He was my age. We spent the night there with him."

Vincent Impallomeni
C Co., 63rd Infantry Regt.

<u>Elsewhere in the Pacific Theater</u>

Following a four-month bombing campaign, U.S. Marine and Army divisions landed on Okinawa on April 1 in the largest amphibious invasion of the war. Subsequent fighting would be the most costly in terms of casualties in the Pacific war. U.S. carrier planes located and sunk the Japanese super-battleship Yamato, which had been dispatched to attack U.S. forces on Okinawa.

In April servicemen received the sad news that President Franklin Roosevelt had died. Less than a month later, half a world away, Germany surrendered, ending the war in Europe. Supplies previously slated for finishing the war in Europe begin pouring into the Philippines as the U.S. started gearing up for the massive invasion of the Japanese home islands.

Word passed down the line that the Germans had surrendered and the war in Europe was over. Well, I thought, that's nice. But we're still fighting over here. I don't think anyone gave it more than a passing thought in their foxholes in the Luzon jungles.

When we were patrolling in the Zigzag pass area we ran into a lot of Negritos, black natives who were quite short. But we didn't have anyone with us that could speak their dialect. Finally we found a Filipino guerrilla that could communicate with them. "Tell them we need their help. Find out what they want." He said they wanted salt. We had tons of salt tablets. The Army stocked us up pretty well with them. But if you took them and started to sweat the salt would come out and soak into your fatigues. So I had whole boxes of the stuff to spare.

One of the Negritos asked through our interpreter if I would like a nice bow and arrow. I told him that it would be hard to get it back home. But I made the deal with him. I gave him a bunch of salt tablets and he gave me a little bow and arrow. He tried to teach me to shoot with it. He was really accurate with it, but I gave up trying to do anything with it.

There were a lot of these little monkeys running around the area. We had tried to catch one to have as a pet, but the little guys were too fast for us. So I asked another Negrito if he could catch one of the monkeys. I told him I wanted a small one and that I would give him a box of salt tablets. I gave him the salt tablets and he motioned for me to stay back.

He shimmied up a coconut tree and pulled a coconut. Then he shimmied back down to the ground and cut the top off the coconut with a machete. He put something into the hollow of the coconut and put it down on the ground near where the monkeys were. It didn't take long for a bunch of little monkeys to come around to investigate the coconut. One stuck his hand inside. He couldn't pull it out but he refused to let go of whatever he had a hold of inside that coconut. The

Negrito went over, picked up the monkey, and brought it over to me. The monkey was wiggling around. I took one of the extra shoelaces I had for my canvas boots, made a little loop and tied it around him.

The monkey finally let go of the coconut and we kept the little guy around for a couple of weeks. It was nice having something to care for and dote on beside your weapons. But then the Japs really started throwing it at us and I was afraid the poor little guy would get killed. So I cut him loose and let him go. "Go ahead, you're free," I said. He looked at me for a moment then scampered off into the brush. I felt sort of sad, but that was the right thing to do for the little fella.

> *"One town we liberated next to the mountains had some headhunters. These guys don't lie, because they bring back the heads of those they kill as proof... These headhunters had bows and arrows for hunting... Some of our boys picked up their bows just to see if they could aim with them. Our boys could only pull the string back three or four inches. That's as far as they could pull it. Then the headhunters were asked to demonstrate. They pulled the string back ten or twelve inches more. They had bands around their arms up by their shoulders to keep from pulling their muscles out. They were powerful people."*
> Vernon Kahl
> C Co., 20th Infantry Regt.

In June I came down with hepatitis. I thought I was just turning yellow from the Atabrine, but I started urinating brown and my fingernails had turned yellow. I hadn't touched any of the fuzzy wuzzies, so I didn't know what it was. Doc Mullins took one look at me and told me to report to the field hospital. The 6th Infantry Division field hospital was pretty typical of field hospitals on Luzon. It was 12 to 15 cots in a large tent. Wounded men were separated from the sick.

I slept on a cot that was covered with mosquito netting because they were pretty bad there. The hospital served up three meals a day, fresh meat, fresh milk, ice cream. I hadn't had fresh meat since we landed. But when you get hepatitis you lose your appetite. I saw the food and I wanted to say, no I just can't do it. Anything I ate made me nauseous. The guy next to me had malaria and he said he would eat it. The orderlies told me I had to eat; that was the only way I would get better. "Force yourself or you're not going to get cured."

I couldn't figure out why the food was going to make me well and not some pills. They told me that hepatitis was a liver disease and the food they were giving me had specific proteins and other nutrients that would help me recover. I got milk and I got cold water, which was very unusual. After about ten days I was well enough to start walking around. The docs said that I would be out of there in a few days, and that's exactly what happened. Two weeks after reporting to the hospital I was back with my squad.

The regiment was moving north up Highway 4. Well, highway might be a bit of an exaggeration. It was little more than a narrow, winding road hardly wide enough in most places for traffic to travel in both directions at the same time. It went up and down through thickly-terrained hills. We were headed for the Ibulao river bridgehead.

"In late June, 3rd Battalion moved into the Cagayan Valley where we came across a lot of Igorot natives. They wore only a G-strings and carried blow guns with which they shot darts using their mouths. They were very friendly and gave us information on Japanese troop strength. They grew rice in paddies that were more than 2000 years old in leveled

mountain terraces. They also grew a root like a sweet
potato and hunted wild animals, chiefly boar."
  C. B. Griggs
  K Co., 1st Infantry Regt.

While we were up there we received some new .50-caliber machine guns. But we had very little ammunition for them. They were Air Corps style with the ammunition in links rather than the belts we were used to. Lt. Allen said, "What do they expect us to do with these? When are they going to send us ammunition?"

I volunteered to go down to the airfield where the guns probably came from, and see what I could do. After all, I was experienced in trading with the Air Corps. Allen told me to grab a jeep and go down to the airfield. "See what you can do," he said.

So I grabbed some Jap rifles, some helmets, mess kits, and other assorted trade goods and went down to the airstrip. It wasn't far because we had the pursuit planes providing us with air support.

I found an Air Corps noncom and told him that I needed .50-caliber ammunition and had goods to trade. Two other noncoms took me over to a big ditch where they were burying belts of ammunition. They were short belts. When the planes came back from a mission, if they didn't finish shooting all their belts the ground crew would take out the used portions and link the unused ammo together. When I came around they were burying the short belts because they had a large enough supply of regular ammunition. I said I would take all I could carry, and the two Air Corps noncoms loaded up the jeep with so much ammunition that the back sunk down. Before I left they gave me some tools that we would need to separate the links and join the belts.

When I got back we linked up some of the belts and fired off a bunch. We must have fired off 5000 rounds. It was sort of weird. Here folks back home were saving nickels and dimes to buy war bonds, and over here everything was expendable. Those bullets probably cost 50 cents apiece and we were just firing them with no discernable purpose. And at the airstrip they were burying thousands upon thousands of them.

On July 12 we caught up with elements of the 63rd Regiment at the Ibulao River. We crossed the Ibulao and continued pushing the Japs north. And the Japs kept counterattacking. Supplies became a problem because of the rugged terrain we were moving through and the extended nature of our supply lines. We reached the town of Banaue on August 4 and patrolled the Banaue-Ducligan area to root out the remaining Japanese.

One morning near Banaue Johnson, the guy who had been collecting Japanese gold teeth, woke up screaming. He was frantic. "They're biting me. They're biting me," he screamed.

"Who?" I asked, trying to calm him down. "Who's biting you?"

"The teeth," he said. "They're biting me." He pushed the box of teeth away. There must have been a couple of hundred in there. "I don't want them anymore. Here you take them."

"Oh no," I said. "I don't want them." I figured if they got to him, I didn't want them getting to me. He tried to give them to the other guys but no one wanted any part of them.

We turned him in and they took him away to the rear. We didn't see him again. I don't know what ever happened to the teeth. Maybe one of the guys took them after all. I didn't care. I certainly didn't want them.

We had another guy go a little loco toward the end. One day he came up to me carrying a box of rocks, the kind that you find in streambeds. He offered to sell me one for $50.00, saying that it was a diamond. I told him it was only a stream rock, but he was adamant that it was a diamond. I told him to go see Vissher. He knew about gemstones. A couple of days later the guys in his tent kicked him out for acting bizarre. Eventually he got sent back to the rear too. We never heard from him again either.

There were lots of times when guys were on the verge of losing it. Sometimes a guy who had been through hell without it fazing him would suddenly say that he wasn't going to make it through the next one. When someone said that I'd tell him, "You're not going to make it if you keep up like this. Just lay flat when the counterattack comes and be in a position where you can fire your weapon."

There was a replacement sergeant from the 32nd Division who had been wounded, I think at Buna. When he got out of the hospital he got transferred to us with a bunch of other noncoms since we were short. He said, "I got it once. I was lucky. But I don't think I'm going to make it through the war. I'm going to die in the next counterattack."

"Don't say that," I said. "I need you."

"God needs me more than you do," he replied. He was transferred out a little while later. He was starting to go a little psycho.

You never could tell which replacements were going to make it. At first everyone figured they would, of course. You never quite get used to getting replacements, all green without any combat experience, and before you get to know them, they're dead. I used to tell them, "There's the machine gun, I'm in back of the gun. You start digging your slit trench alongside, and make sure you're far enough away from the next guy that you don't ruin his hole." It continued to amaze me that the replacements looked to me as an experienced veteran. It had been little more than a year since we hit the beach at Maffin Bay. Combat, especially in the Pacific, changed you pretty quickly.

I never had premonitions or feelings of impending death. But my mother did come to me. I would always see her before a big counterattack, never when the going was easy. Once I actually saw a vision of her and she talked to me. I told a couple of the guys about it and that's when they thought that I might be starting to go a little nuts. So I never talked about it again.

Rumor had it that Yamashita was trying to evacuate to the north coast, but we had sunk the submarine sent to pick him up. So he was holed up in the mountains with the remainder of his army. We knew he was trapped. He knew he was trapped. But that didn't stop the counterattacks. They still fought furiously. Surrender still was not an option. It all seemed like a terribly senseless waste of life.

> "This drive [to destroy enemy troops south of Kiangan] was followed by a seven-hour armistice on July 24, devised to allow the enemy elements to surrender in comparative safety.
> "The armistice was publicized by leaflets dropped or fired into enemy territory and by public address broadcasts from a low lying cub. The truce resulted in no surrenders. Instead, artillery observers near the objective hill could see the Nips scurrying about preparing more positions and camouflage."
> Robert Damm
> 1st Field Artillery

While we were up at Banaue, Irv Cohen, the company clerk who had contracted typhus at Sansapor, finally rejoined the unit after spending about six months in the hospital. When he got back they put him in my section. I knew he was another Jewish guy, but up to that time I really hadn't spent much time with him and didn't know very much about him.

As a child I had lived with my Aunt Jeannette and Uncle Louis for a time when my father was traveling. Then I lived with my Aunt Bella. I also lived for a time with Max Abrams, a really friendly guy who took me in for a while. He was a good friend of my mother, Sadel. They were both English and belonged to the English Club in Chicago. Living with my different aunts and uncles wasn't working out too well and Max offered to take me in. I stayed with him for about a year.

I mentioned to Irv that I was from Chicago. Irv was from Kansas City but said he had an uncle that lived in Chicago. So we just started talking. He said his uncle lived in the Rogers Park neighborhood, which was where I was from, and said that he had a big gas station there. I asked him if his uncle's name was Max Abrams and he said yes, it was. Talk about coincidence!

My squad was getting ready to go out on patrol and Irv asked to go out with us. We knew the war would be over soon. We heard that a new superbomb had been dropped on one of the big Japanese cities, but we didn't know which one. Then a couple of days later we heard another one had been dropped. The Air Corps had started dropping leaflets on the Japanese telling them to surrender. I tried to convince Irv that it wasn't a good idea.

> *The world's first atomic bomb was dropped on Hiroshima by the B29, Enola Gay, flying out of Tinian in the Marianas, on August 6, 1945. The Japanese, however, were not moved enough to give up the fight. A second atomic bomb was dropped on Nagasaki by the B29, Bockscar, on August 9. The second bomb finally moved the Emperor to seek peace.*

"You don't have to go," I said to Irv. "You were in the hospital for six months and you don't look too good. You're not strong and it's rough territory where we're going. We could have a cease-fire at any time."

"I want to see combat before the war is over," he said. "Even if it's only one patrol."

"I highly advise against it," I said. But he was adamant. A couple of the other guys quickly volunteered to have Irv take their place. So I relented.

We marched into the hills near Banaue. On the way we crossed some little stream on foot. It wasn't much and we waded across. It was drizzling on us, but what we didn't know was that further up in the hills there was a rainstorm. About two hours later we were on the way back, but in that short time the stream had turned into a torrent. It had grown to about 25 or 30 feet wide.

We talked it over and decided to try to cross. We had two Filipino natives helping us and they crossed first, using their spears for support against the water and slippery rocks. Sergeant Nursky followed, then four or five more of us. Bradigan crossed carrying a machine gun receiver and tripod. He got almost all the way across, then looked like he was stuck. Glen Davis stepped out into the water and Bradigan handed the equipment to him. Bradigan fell and we yelled, "Come on Yank, get up." He did and made it across.

Irv was next. He made it about halfway across, then lost his balance and fell into the torrent. The water carried him over this little falls and then the river disappeared around a curve to the left. Nursky ran along the bank trying to reach him, but the water was too swift. Irv disappeared.

We decided not to try to get any more men across. The rest of the guys stayed on the far side of the stream for the night. I think we all had a sleepless night that night. We were worried about a buddy. The next morning, the stream had shrunk to where it was safe to cross. We returned to Battalion and were in the process of forming a search party when a group of about eight natives came into camp carrying Irv's body on a stretcher. Whenever they found one of our men, they would bring him into camp and we would give them food as thanks.

I looked at Irv with great sadness. "Irv," I said. "I told you, you didn't have to go."

That same day the Air Corps was dropping leaflets in Japanese saying that Emperor Hirohito had declared a surrender. We heard it over the radio. The formal cease-fire was announced at 17:20 (5:20 p.m.) on August 15.

> *"We were in the Cagayan Valley. An Air Corps plane came in real low. We thought it was going to drop rations. Instead it dropped leaflets saying the war was over. But the Japs were still fighting."*
> Gary Mendoza
> A Co., 1st Infantry Regt.

> *"It was about 9:00 in the morning when I was told the war was over. We were all sleeping because we'd had a night attack the night before. The first sergeant came around and kicked the bottom of my feet. He said, 'Sergeant Kahl, get your boys together, pack up your pack. The war is over! We're going home!'"*
> Vernon Kahl
> C Co., 20th Infantry Regt.

> *"We were to attack the adjacent hill the next day. We had gotten machine gun and mortar fire from there, about two-thirds of the way up the Cagayan Valley in the mountains. One of us stayed on guard during that night, two hours on, two off. Our radio was at Battalion HQ and Battalion would inform us of the situation along the battalion line. The message we got during the night was, 'Cease all offensive action, fire only if fired upon.' But we were wary.*
>
> *"By daylight, the captain told us that the Japanese had said that they would surrender, but wanted to keep the Empire. As it turned out there*

was some trouble with translation and this was changed from Empire to Emperor. Near noon, it began to sink in. If it was true it meant no more digging, no more field rations. No more guard duty. Could it be?

"We heard that a bomb had been dropped, but we could not comprehend an atomic bomb. I think I felt relief that things would be better. No more attacks, no more advances. I was going home. Suddenly my mind saw the ones we would never see again, the ones that wouldn't be going home. I couldn't believe that I would actually miss the Army. I knew it was a part of us forever."
      C. B. Griggs
      K Co., 1st Infantry Regt.

The End of the War in the Pacific

The Japanese accepted unconditional surrender on August 14, 1945. The U.S. began landing troops to begin the occupation of Japan on August 29. Formal surrender ceremonies were held onboard the battleship Missouri, anchored in Tokyo Bay, on September 2. The most devastating war in the history of the world was over.

In defeating Japan, Germany and their allies, the U.S. had suffered one million casualties, 400,000 of them deaths. Estimates of the total death toll on all sides worldwide vary widely. Estimates of military deaths range from 20 to 25 million and estimates of civilian deaths range from 36 to 52 million.

9. End Game

Cease fire. What beautiful words. The word was passed down the line on any radio communications that we had. We all started firing our guns in the air just to use up ammunition and celebrating that the war was finally over. Everyone started laughing. We were up at Banaue where the water was coming out of the mountains and the only thing we had to drink was coffee. I couldn't believe it at first. I had made it. I was going home.

Of course a lot of the Japs didn't believe it at first. They thought it was some sort of trick. But eventually they all surrendered. They came out of the hills and we were shocked to see how many of them were still up there, ready to fight. The Army wanted us to round up all the Japanese that we could because they were afraid if they fell into the hands of the guerillas, they would be tortured or killed. We especially wanted to corral the officers. Yamashita and his officers eventually came out of the hills carrying a white flag. The highest-ranking American officer there was a captain, but Yamashita made it known that he wouldn't surrender to a captain. He would only surrender to a high-ranking officer. A colonel came up and accepted Yamashita's surrender.

> *"Third Battalion was camped outside Bagabag, about 100 yards off the main highway. One afternoon, about 50 trucks stopped and allowed their Japanese prisoners to relieve themselves. We went down to talk to them and found that some could speak English pretty well. It turns out that they were in the unit that we were preparing to attack before the cease*

fire. The numbers they talked about were staggering. They reported that there were around 35,000 soldiers there. We had been told that there were only a few hundred!"
      C. B. Griggs
      K Co., 1st Infantry Regt.

No Japs surrendered to my platoon. Other units rounded them up and trucks took them from Banaue to a stockade. We stayed up at Banaue for about a week after the cease-fire. Then they sent some trucks to pick us up. The engineers had already built a road through the mountain pass there and it was an uneventful trip down to San Fernando North where we had a big replacement and supply dump.

We were shocked when we pulled in to San Fernando North. There was a massive stockpile of brand new equipment, guns, vehicles and ammunition as far as you could see. It was being readied for the next invasion, which was supposed to be Honshu in the Japanese home islands. Word there was that the brass expected up to 90% casualties the first week of the invasion. I know there has been a lot of talk back and forth as to whether or not we should have deployed the atomic bombs on Japan, whether or not it was morally justified. Let me tell you, as one of the men who might have been fighting in that invasion, there was absolutely no doubt in my mind. Especially after what we heard about the fanatical and tenacious resistance of the Japanese on Okinawa, I, and everyone I knew in the Army over there, was sure grateful that invasion never came to pass.

Operation Downfall, the massive invasion of the Japanese home islands, was well into the final planning stages when the war ended. Japan still had a sizeable fighting force protecting the home islands

and civilians were instructed in how to resist and kill
Allied troops. The campaign was projected to have
casualties numbering in the millions.

The Army had us unloading new jeeps for a couple of
weeks. The Jeeps came in big wooden crates and we gave the
wood to the Filipinos. The old equipment, the stuff that we
had used, was loaded up on ships and dumped into the
ocean. I looked at the massive stockpile of ammunition that
was being saved for the invasion and thought, boy we could
have used some of that up in the mountains. Maybe we
wouldn't have lost so many guys toward the end.

The guys that had enough points were going to go
home. I tallied up my points and I had more than enough to
be discharged. But it didn't do me any good. They told me
they didn't have a replacement for me. So I had to wait.

After a couple of weeks they gave out some ten-day
passes to Manila, or what was left of it. The pass was for three
guys and a sergeant in a jeep. They gave us each $15.00
supplementary pay, which was about 30 pesos. And that
wouldn't go very far.

The four of us drove in to Manila. It was pretty well
blown up. Yamashita had pulled out of the city when the
Americans approached it, but one of his senior officers stayed
behind, determined to defend the city to the death. The
ensuing battle all but destroyed the city.

There were a lot of little kids on the streets. Some of
them had been wounded in the fighting. There were still
some parts that were OK, but most of the city had been
devastated. I remember that the Chinese section still had a lot
of its statues.

When   General   Douglas   MacArthur
evacuated from Manila in December 1941, he
withdrew his forces and declared Manila and open
city. Declaring a city open was a way of sending a

*message to the attacking forces that the city would
not be defended in the hopes that its buildings and
citizens would be spared. The Americans withdrew
and, after a few air raids, the Japanese marched in.*

*When General Tomoyuki Yamashita
evacuated from Manila in 1945, he gave orders that
his forces be withdrawn and only the bridges be
blown. He left, but one of his subordinates, Admiral
Sanji, refused to give up the city, instead vowing to
defend it to the death. Sanji set up defenses and the
resulting fierce urban battles, often house to house
fighting, nearly destroyed the city. One thousand
Americans were killed. Twelve thousand Japanese,
the entire garrison, were killed. And approximately
100,000 Filipino civilians were killed by bombings,
crossfire, and massacres by retreating Japanese.*

We drove around town for a while trying to decide
what to do. One of the guys, Bull Torres, said he had an idea
to pick up a little spending cash. He got out of the jeep and
started smearing axle grease on the identification on the
bumpers so no one could see where we were from. Then he
asked me how much ammunition I had. I told him I didn't
have much, but there were a couple of grenades in the jeep.
He said he would take two of them.

I didn't know what he had planned, but I figured
there was no sense endangering any innocent people...or us.
So before giving them to him I emptied the gunpowder out
into the street. Torres winked and said he was going to hold
up a whorehouse. Everyone was scared of grenades, because
they were wicked, and he figured all he had to do was flash
them around. While the rest of us stayed in the jeep, Bull ran
into this whorehouse. He held up the grenades and pulled
the pins.

I heard him yell, "This is a stick up. Give me all your
pesos!"

The Filipino pimp yelled, "No Joe. You screw girl, no charge."

Torres said he didn't want a girl. He wanted money and he would blow the place up if he didn't get it. Most of the Americans in there were rear echelon guys. They saw this guy with grenades with the pins pulled out, and they came running out in various stages of undress and scattered. The next thing I knew Bull came running out holding a bunch of pesos. He jumped in the jeep and we drove off.

We scored maybe a thousand pesos. We split it up and had a good time. We hooked up with some girls and drank too much basi. We ate pretty well, too, although we stayed away from the meat. It was mostly from water buffaloes. We stuck to chicken, which was a lot safer. It was just the four of us, but we ran into some of our other guys who were there. They wondered where we had gotten the money. We didn't say.

The money lasted a couple of days. After it ran out we went to some of the other outfits that were in town to get food. We traded with some Filipinos too.

When our pass was up we returned to San Fernando North. Before we took the jeep back we cleaned off the bumpers so the identification showed. Soon after we returned we got new fatigues and they ran us through a physical check at a field hospital. We were wondering why we were getting all this attention. Maybe they were sending us home after all. But no, we got orders to go to Korea to disarm the Japanese there.

We loaded up on transports and arrived at the port of Inchon in late September. You had to go in at high tide because at low tide you couldn't even get near the docks, there was so much difference in the water lines.

Our job in Korea was to round up all the Japanese soldiers there and process them for return to Japan. They had all gotten the word that Japan had surrendered and we didn't have any problems with them, not in my unit at least. We rounded them up, tagged them with their name and what town they were from in Japan, and put them in a stockade. We took any weapons they had and threw them in a big pile. Later everything was loaded up on ships and dumped into the ocean. We separated the officers from the enlisted men for transport back to Japan.

> *"We were being transferred to a new post up near Andong. My section was assigned to be an advanced party to go up ahead of time to where the battalion was going to set up. There were big barns there and supply had dumped a big supply of cots in front of them.*
>
> *"I knew how many men were in the company and I knew which barn was designated for H Co. The rest of the company was coming up later in the day and I figured I would have our barn all set up for them. So I told the guys to grab the cots and set up the barn, machine guns on one side, mortars on the other. Some of the guys, including Leonard, figured they were going to take it easy and wander around. They got pissed. 'Well who the hell told you to do that?' they asked. 'Well nobody,' I said. And I just told them to do it. The other companies had to set up in the dark but we were all set up when our guys got there. I don't think Leonard ever forgave me for that."*
>
> Mark Bradigan
> H Co., 1st Infantry Regt.

While I was in Korea I got word that I was going to be promoted to staff sergeant. But almost immediately following that news, I got word that I would be returning to the States soon, so it wouldn't make any difference. I didn't really care at that point. I just wanted to go home.

Every morning, at reveille, the first sergeant called out the names of the guys who would be going home. Each day I waited for my name to be called. When your name wasn't called, you just went about your daily business. Finally he called my name. "Your orders have come in," he said. "Pack up all your belongings. You have a replacement."

I was finally going home.

To say I was excited would be a massive understatement. I certainly didn't want to stay in Korea any longer than I had to. I'd done my job and I'd had my fill of Army life. And the Koreans weren't too happy to have us around anyway. All I thought about was getting home as quickly as I could.

It was pretty hard saying good-bye to the guys that didn't have enough points to go home. They were happy for you, but I knew that they were also feeling bad. After all, I'd been in their place until that morning. A full company was around 200 men, a battalion around a thousand. They had called around 20 from my company and about 60 or 70 from the battalion.

> *"Each day, one or two men would leave. They would come by your tent, start some small talk, then say something like, 'So long, I'll be seeing you.' Then he would start to walk away. After a few steps he'd come back. 'If so and so ever gets out of the hospital, tell him I would like to see him.' After another attempt to leave he'd come back and say, 'If you ever come through, wherever, look me up, and I'll do the same for you.' Some would come back four or five times, then as he choked up he would say, 'I've got to go, they're waiting for me.' And he would be gone."*
>
> C. B. Griggs
> K Co., 1st Infantry Regt.

The plan was to have a bunch of us trucked over to Seoul and then to a seaport where we would board an aircraft carrier that would take us back to the States. But when we got to Seoul the weather was pretty bad and the aircraft carrier didn't make it over from Japan. Rather than wait for the carrier, they put us up in a tent city for the night. They were bringing in an APA to take us home. But it was going to leave from Inchon, the port with the crazy tides, so they said they would probably be waking us up in the middle of the night so we could get down to Inchon, load up, and depart before the tide shifted.

And that's exactly what we did. We loaded up on the APA. To my surprise, the ship looked relatively empty. I thought it would be packed like our transport coming over. But there were only about 500 of us on a ship rigged with 3000 berths.

One of the sailors leading us to our berths said, "Well at least you'll eat well. We have lots of food onboard." Then he asked, "Who knows how to carve meat, because everyone onboard has to have a job and we need a meat carver."

For some reason I said, "I'm a meat carver."

"Ok, you're attached to the galley," he said.

"What's that?" I asked.

"That's the ship's kitchen," he said. "You go there and talk to the head chef."

I went down to the galley and found the head chef. He said, "We've got lots of turkey onboard so we'll be serving lots of turkey. Do you know how to carve a turkey?"

"Of course," I said.

I had never carved a turkey in my life and didn't know the first thing about it. Somehow, I muddled my way through it. By the end of the trip I was a pretty good turkey carver.

We got underway, and the first thing I noticed was that we were traveling alone. The war was over so there was no need for a convoy. The other thing I noticed was that we traveled with all of our lights on. That was different too.

The trip from Korea to Seattle was supposed to take nine days. But out in the Pacific we ran into rough storms. At times the ship was tossed around like a cork. One of our motors burned out. We came across a liberty ship that was stuck because its motors had burned out. So we took it in tow. But it was too heavy for us and it burned out our motor too.

We were about a hundred miles out of Seattle and we were taking on water. I thought that would be a hell of an ending if I made it all the way through the war and wound up drowning a hundred miles from home. Since there were only 500 of us being transported the ship was riding a little high in the water. We all went back to the stern of the boat to put more weight there and that seemed to relieve the flooding a little.

Two ocean-going tugs came out to meet us. We dropped the cable to the liberty ship and each tug took one ship in tow. They towed us to Seattle, but they couldn't take us all the way in. We grabbed our duffle bags and loaded into lifeboats for a rather non-glorious entry back into the United States. But we were home. How good it felt to step onto the good old USA again. When we landed they told us we would be spending the night in Seattle. They pointed us to the local USO where we could get some food, and told us to report back in the morning. They gave us $15.00 in case we wanted to do anything else.

The very first thing I did was to find a phone and call my father. He was overjoyed and told me he would wire money to me by Western Union so I could come home right away. I told him that I had to be discharged first and the Army wouldn't think too kindly of me if I disappeared before they processed me out. I told him my first stop was Camp Stoneman, near Seattle.

All of us wanted a nice big steak, but when we got to the USO all they had were the usual sandwiches and coffee.

We found out that there was a good steak house nearby, so a group of us hiked over there and had nice, big fat juicy steak dinners. At that time you could get a good steak dinner for around $5.00, so we even had money left over.

We went back to the USO and slept on the floor. They had taken our duffle bags and put them in a secure location so we didn't have to lug them around with us. The next morning we reclaimed our duffels and they took us to Camp Stoneman. The first thing they did there was give us a physical checkup. It seemed like I got a physical at every darn step along the way. After the physical they issued us all new clothing. Then they asked where we came into the Army, which camp. I said Camp Grant, and they said that's where I would be going back to be discharged from the service.

> *"At the base they told us we had one responsibility. That was to check the bulletin board each morning at 9:00 a.m. The movement of soldiers was posted each day at 8:00 a.m. for the ones leaving 24 hours later. Trains and busses would then take us to separation centers nearest to our homes for discharge. My name appeared on the bulletin board on 15 December. Louisiana, here I come!"*
> C. B. Griggs
> K Co., 1st Infantry Regt.

We loaded up on trains – real coaches this time with seats, no boxcars – for the trip back to Illinois. They served one or two meals a day. Spam sandwiches. When meal time came around we joked, "Here comes Camp Spam." We had so much Spam I vowed never to eat it again.

We got to Camp Grant near Rockford, Illinois, on December 22 and the first thing they did was – you guessed it – give us a physical. Then they took away the clothes that we had gotten at Stoneman and gave us all brand new clothes again. Since we were so close to Christmas, they gave us a pass to go home, but we had to report back the day after Christmas to continue our processing or we would be considered AWOL.

I called my father and told him I was coming home, but that I had to go back after Christmas. I jumped on the train for the 90-minute ride to Union Station in Chicago. My father was waiting at the station along with my stepmother, Ann, my brother, Eddie, and my half brother, Marvin. We were all so happy to see each other after two years. They all looked the same, but I felt like I had changed. My father gave me a big hug. He never said anything, but I knew that he thought that I wasn't going to make it back.

We drove straight home. It was late and after a little talk, we went to bed. I had to sleep in the same bed as my brother, Eddie, but it was a bed. A real bed. Even though it was very late, and I'd had a long day, I didn't fall sleep right away. For the first time since the war's end I thought about all the guys that wouldn't be coming home, and the guys that didn't make it back in one piece.

It's funny, the thoughts that pop into your head. I thought about this one guy from New Mexico, a replacement, who was assigned to my squad on Luzon. He came in late in the afternoon. He didn't have the faintest idea of what to do. I told him to start digging a slit trench in back of the machine gun. I told him to get it done quickly because it was already 3:00 and by 5:00 the Japs would be shelling us. The machine gun was next to a tree and he started digging. Suddenly the Japs started shelling us. I pushed him into my hole and I jumped in on top of him. I didn't realize it but my legs were spread apart. We got a tree burst. I didn't get hit but the burst took off his foot. It was his first day. Well, if I hadn't pushed him into the hole he would have been killed. This way he only lost a foot. If I would have had my feet together it would have been me losing a foot. And at any time in combat, a stray bullet here, a mortar on a slightly different trajectory there, or a piece of shrapnel flying out at a little different angle, and I wouldn't be lying next to my brother in a warm cozy bed.

I reported back to Camp Grant the day after Christmas, as ordered. On three different days I got three different physicals. After one I had an interview with a WAC nurse.

"How do you feel?" she asked.

"I feel great." I thought that's what they would want to hear.

"No you don't," she said. You were wounded three times. You must be in pain."

"No," I said. "I just want to get out of here."

She was typing onto my form as she spoke. "Don't worry about it. We'll get you home." I didn't realize it at the time but her comments would get me a little extra money on my GI pension.

It took the Army two more weeks to finish with me. I finally got my discharge on January 14, 1946, two and a half years and a world away from when I had enlisted in August of 1943. I was finally home.

I had fought in New Guinea and the Philippines. Whether by divine providence or sheer dumb luck, I had survived a brutal war fought in unbelievably hellish conditions. So many others weren't as fortunate. I had seen things that are disturbing to me to this day, more than 60 years later. I had earned three Purple Hearts and three Bronze Star commendations. I am proud of the part I played in winning the war, and I am so immensely proud of the men I served with in the 1st Infantry Regiment and the 6th Infantry Division.

Epilogue

Sergeant Leonard J. Gordon was discharged from the U.S. Army on January 14, 1946. He had served 28 months with 19 of those being in the Pacific Theater of Operations. He returned home to Chicago and began the adjustment to civilian life. Like many returning GIs he decided to take advantage of the GI bill and go to college. His father did the graduation photographs for Loyola University and got him an interview with the admissions department. The advisor asked him what field of study he wanted to go into. Leonard wasn't sure; he hadn't given it much thought to that point. The advisor recommended a course in economics.

So Leonard studied economics for a year, but found it not to his liking. He left Loyola, got married and opened a small neighborhood store with his brother-in-law, Al. The business was moderately successful, and a few of his 6th Infantry buddies dropped in from time to time. But after a few years they sold the store. Leonard took a job with a camera distributor and found his true passion. He rose steadily through the ranks, working for several camera companies. It is perhaps an indication of the man the boy had become that just 20 years after the war he took a sales management job with a Japanese camera company, working with the same people with whom we had once been bitter enemies. He made numerous trips to Japan and enjoyed working with his Japanese colleagues. The high point of his career was with Canon Camera Co. where he was vice-president of sales for North America. He retired, eventually moving from Chicago to Scottsdale, Arizona.

A Funeral

March 12, 2009

The mahogany casket sits on a rolling bier in the front of the small hushed chapel. An American flag is draped over it, the stars and blue field at the head. A member of a military honor guard stands at attention at each side. Family and friends hold back tears as a World War II veteran, a former noncommissioned officer wearing a VFW garrison cap, approaches the podium next to the casket to deliver a eulogy for a decorated fellow veteran of that conflict.

It is a small service, many of his family and friends already having gone before him. The speaker salutes Leonard James Gordon, Sergeant, Company H, 1st Infantry Regiment, 6th Infantry Division. He speaks of honor, of patriotism, of commitment. He speaks of putting on the uniform of the United States Army and how Leonard and all who served with him and before him, and all who would serve after him are prepared to die for the flag now covering him. He speaks of service and fighting in New Guinea and Luzon. He speaks of heroism, Purple Hearts and Bronze Stars. He concludes by pronouncing that Sergeant Gordon has completed his final assignment.

A bugler at the rear of the chapel sounds Taps. The mournful tones seem to hang in the air even after the bugler sounds the last extended note. Then the honor guard solemnly removes the flag from the casket and folds it according to tradition with crisp but smoothly-measured movements. One clutches the flag, now folded into a tight triangle with four stars facing out, to his chest. All who served in the U.S. armed forces are called forward and they reverently pass the flag from one to the next. Finally it is presented to his son. The honor guard then rolls the casket down the center aisle and out of the chapel to the waiting hearse.

Later, at the gravesite, an officer stands off to the side with the three-member firing party, four other World War II veterans. They look as old, or older, than he was. It is unseasonably cold, even for Chicago, and they are all clad in olive-colored military great coats. M1 Garands rest at their sides. They are at ease, but ready. After the religious service concludes the officer calls the squad to attention.

They respond smartly to his terse commands.

"Load." They take position, load a clip and chamber a round.

"Ready." They flick off their safeties.

"Aim." They shoulder their weapons and aim upward at 45-degrees into the air over the gravesite.

"Fire." They fire a round in perfect unison, the sharp retort shattering the silence.

They fire two more rounds for a total of three, a custom derived from days when opposing armies would declare a temporary truce to clear their dead from the battlefield. Each would fire three volleys to signify that the task was complete and hostilities were to resume.

"Cease firing." They return to attention with their weapons held at port arms.

"Present arms." They hold their weapons forward in present arms as Taps sounds once again, the salute even more heart-wrenching than before. After the bugler finishes the officer gives the final command.

"Order arms." They return to attention, with weapons at port arms.

The cold wind whips their aged faces, but they remain at attention, impervious to the blustery conditions that are already sending many of the mourners back to their cars. They are brothers in arms paying final respects to one of their own, his journey now, at last, complete. It was a journey that started over 65 years earlier on that quiet Sunday in December 1941.

Sources and Acknowledgements

The main source of information for this book was, of course, interviews with Leonard Gordon and several other veterans of the 6th Infantry Division who participated in the New Guinea and Luzon campaigns. Their memories of people, conversations, engagements and events from their days in the army remain amazingly sharp. At times, though, specific dates and locations got a little mixed up after so many years. And in cross-checking their recollections I noticed that, in a few instances, people sometimes were tagged with a wrong name, or placed in a wrong location. When there was any doubt or conflicting information I have made every attempt to reconcile those differences with other sources. Names presented an additional problem because even if they recalled the name of a buddy or officer, etc., they often had no idea how to spell it. So I took my best shot, checking when possible against available records. My apologies if I spelled your name or that of a relative incorrectly, or placed him in an errant location or activity.

I sincerely thank all the 6th Infantry veterans and their families who provided me with supporting information regarding the war in the Pacific. But I especially want to thank Mark Bradigan (H Co., 1st Infantry Regt.), Vincent Impallomeni (C Co., 63rd Infantry Regt.), Leo Hennigan (D Co., 6th Medical Bn.), Milt Galke (E Co., 1st Infantry Regt.), Gary Mendoza (A Co., 1st Infantry Regt.), Robert Damm (1st Field Artillery), and Vernon Kahl (C Co., 20th Infantry Regt.).

And a special thanks to C. B. Griggs (K Co., 1st Infantry Regt.) who allowed me to use information from his memoirs to verify numerous facts and fill in some thin spots in Leonard's story.

In addition to the interviews, much of the supporting historical material was taken from existing sources in print and on the Internet. These sources are listed in the bibliography, but I would like to point out a few that were especially helpful. For the story of the 6th Infantry Division from training in the States to post-combat duties in Korea, *The 6th Infantry Division in World War II* by United States. For a detailed description of the campaigns in New Guinea and the Philippines at the divisional level, *Approach to the Philippines* and *Triumph in the Philippines* by Robert Ross Smith. For an insightful look at the life and thoughts of the combat soldier in World War II, *The Deadly Brotherhood* by John McManus and *Goodbye Darkness* by William Manchester.

Memoirs by other veterans of the 6th Infantry Division include: *Tiki Tiki Rimbo* by Robert Damm, and *Becoming Sergeant Kahl: Lingering Memories of a World War II Vet* by Vernon Kahl.

There are numerous Internet sites covering World War II in the Pacific. Wikipedia
(www.wikipedia.com)
has articles on all major, as well as many minor, engagements. The U.S. Army Center of Military History
(http://www.history.army.mil/html/bookshelves/res mat/ww2apt.html#tab_1)
has links to published material including the Reports of General MacArthur and a description of the Luzon campaign from the Japanese perspective. The Hyperwar site
(http://www.ibiblio.org/hyperwar/USA/)
has links to many detailed histories including those under The War in the Pacific heading where you can find an online version of the books by Robert Ross Smith listed above.

Selected Bibliography

Axelrod, Alan. *The Real History of World War II: a New Look at the Past*. New York, NY: Sterling. 2008.

Bergerud, Eric M. *Touched with Fire: the Land War in the South Pacific*. New York, NY: Viking. 1996.

Bull, Stephen. *World War II Jungle Warfare Tactics*. Oxford, UK: Osprey Pub. 2007.

Bull, Stephen, and Gordon L. Rottman. *Infantry Tactics of the Second World War*. Oxford, UK: Osprey Pub. 2008.

Campbell, James. *The Ghost Mountain Boys: Their Epic March and the Terrifying Battle for New Guinea-- the Forgotten War of the South Pacific*. New York, NY: Crown Publishers. 2007.

Cowdrey, Albert E. *Fighting for Life, American Military Medicine in World War II*. New York, NY. Free Press. 1998.

Damm, Robert. *Tiki Tiki Rimbo*. Bloomington, IN: AuthorHouse. 2008.

Fallen, Tom, and Ray Fallen. *The First Infantry Regiment in World War II*. Chicago, Ill: Adams Press. 1990.

Gailey, Harry. *MacArthur's Victory: The War in New Guinea (1943-1944)*. New York, NY: Presidio Press. 2004.

Green, Michael. *MacArthur in the Pacific: From the Philippines to the Fall of Japan*. San Francisco, CA: Motorbooks International. 1996.

Holzimmer, Kevin C. *General Walter Krueger: Unsung Hero of the Pacific War*. Lawrence, Kansas: University Press of Kansas. 2007.

Kahl, Vernon M., Karolyn Anderson, and Elise Rebecca Kahl. *Becoming Sgt. Kahl: Lingering Memories of a WWII Vet*. Inwood, Iowa: V.M. Kahl. 2002.

Krueger, Walter. *From Down Under to Nippon: the Story of the 6th Army In World War II*. Lawrence, Kansas: Zenger Pub. 1979.

McLogan, Russell E. *Boy Soldier: Coming of Age During World War II*. Reading, MI: Terrus Press. 1998.

Munschauer, John L. *World War II Cavalcade, An Offer I Couldn't Refuse*. Manhattan, KS: Sunflower University Press. 1996.

Prefer, Nathan. *MacArthur's New Guinea Campaign March –August 1944*. Conshohocken, PA. Combined Books. 1995.

Sides, Hampton. *Ghost Soldiers: The Epic Account of World War II's Greatest Rescue Mission*. New York, NY. Anchor Books. 2001.

Smith, Robert Ross. *The Approach to the Philippines*. Washington, D. C.: Office of the Chief of Military History, Dept. of the Army. 1953.

Smith, Robert Ross. *Triumph in the Philippines*. Washington D. C.: Office of the Chief of Military History, Dept. of the Army. 1963.

Spector, Ronald. *Eagle Against the Sun: The American War With Japan*. New York, NY. Knopf Doubleday Publishing Group. 1985.

Steinberg, Rafael. *Return to the Philippines. World War II*. Alexandria, Va: Time-Life Books. 1979.

United States. *6th Infantry Division in World War II*. Washington, D.C.: Infantry Journal Press. 1947

CPSIA information can be obtained at www.ICGtesting.com
Printed in the USA
LVOW121817170113

316152LV00020B/1165/P